VAMPIRE KILLER

A TERRIFYING TRUE STORY OF PSYCHOSIS, MUTILATION AND MURDER

RYAN GREEN

For Helen, Harvey, Frankie and Dougie

Disclaimer

This book is about real people committing real crimes. The story has been constructed by facts but some of the scenes, dialogue and characters have been fictionalised.

Polite Note to the Reader

This book is written in British English except where fidelity to other languages or accents are appropriate. Some words and phrases may differ from US English.

YOUR FREE BOOK IS WAITING

From bestselling author Ryan Green

There is a man who is officially classed as "**Britain's most dangerous prisoner**"

The man's name is Robert Maudsley, and his crimes earned him the nickname "**Hannibal the Cannibal**"

This free book is an exploration of his story...

Get a free copy of ***Robert Maudsley: Hannibal the Cannibal*** when you sign up to join my Reader's Group.

www.ryangreenbooks.com/free-book

CONTENTS

Black by Moonlight

Nevada was a funny old state. Just a step away from the shining lights of Vegas and it became just like everywhere else. One step further into the shadows and the whole world became dark and weird in the starlight.

Out here by the Pyramid Lake Reservation, it was always too quiet. Working in the Bureau of Indian Affairs was a dull affair for the most part. Petty crimes, drink and drugs. Deportation back and forth between the authority of the Paiute Nation and the State was the biggest job, and even that barely filled a day a month. The rest of the time, there was just the open road and the roll of hours, day after day. The phone never rang until all the excitement was over. In the city, a cop would dread domestic disturbances and gunfights, but out here in the middle of nowhere, they feared the silence. Evil deeds were done in the dark, and few folk ever spoke of them. There were no missing people on the reservation. No murderers or thieves or any of the average sort of criminal. There were just familiar faces that suddenly weren't there the next time a visit was required. The mob and their code of silence might have kept a hold on Vegas all this time, but they were rank amateurs compared to the Indians out on their reservations. Fear and hate of the police were bred into them, the latest repressed generation in a long and bloody history.

Tonight the asphalt shone in the light of a full moon, even where the full-beam of their headlights didn't reach – a long curve of light in the dark of the night. Tonight, of all nights, the phone had rung, calling the Bureau men out of the tentative safety of their coffee at a diner and into the nebulous dark where anything might be waiting for them.

Few enough things troubled the Paiute enough to call in a complaint. After years of political clashes and less than equitable treatment under the law, the police were the enemy, and for most of them, the skeleton crew of Indian Affairs was the face of that oppression – the only lawmen to dare step foot inside the reservation.

Unless the locals were completely certain that whatever was going on could not somehow be turned around and blamed on them, they wouldn't even pick up the phone. Which meant that whoever was playing the fool down on the beach by Pyramid Lake was going to be a white man. At this time of night, it was almost certain to be somebody poaching fish. The Paiute made most of their income doling out fishing licenses to tourists, and they took anyone sneaking around and trying to catch fish in their lake without one pretty seriously. More than once, the Bureau boys had come out to the lake first thing in the morning to help some sheepish fool find the wheels of their car, which had become mysteriously detached while they were out fishing through the night, and direct them to the office where they could sheepishly pay for their license for the day.

If there had ever been a fisherman that required more than that to scare them off, then the Paiute had done a good enough job of hiding the body and car that no investigation had ever been opened. The call tonight wasn't just unusual, it was the first that either man in the Bureau could ever remember having received outside of office hours.

The pick-up truck that they discovered around the curve of the lake had all of its wheels attached, but that was about all that could be said in favour of it. It loomed up abruptly out of the lake's thin night fog, an incongruous lump on the smooth sand at the side of the road.

It took a moment to decipher what they were looking at without daylit colour to rely on. The truck hadn't felt the gentle touch of soap or sponge for many a month; a thick patina of sand and dirt coated it halfway up its sides. It was only after staring out through their windshield for a solid minute that the Bureau boys managed to identify the truck by its silhouette as a Ford Ranchero.

Despite all this, neither man was compelled to arm themselves or even worry too much as they approached the vehicle. It was only when they rounded the side and realised that the driver's door was hanging open that their vigilance kicked up a notch. The interior light had been left on, draining the car battery and highlighting the desolation that had been left within. A heap of rubbish was crammed into the footwell on the passenger side, pushed down until it was flat. The mess on the passenger seat was not so well contained, sprawling out in every direction. It was such a confusing mess of fast-food wrappers, discarded cigarette packs, and long dried-up bottles of liquor that it took the police a solid couple of minutes of investigation before they came across anything more concerning than what appeared to be a car some homeless alcoholic was living in.

The first worry was a rifle. Only the barrel jutted up out of the morass, and it was slim enough that it took a couple of passes before the iron-sights on the end could be identified correctly. The barrel opened out into a hole just big enough to slip a fingertip inside, were they inclined to contaminate their evidence with their prints. It was a .22 calibre rifle in amongst all this chaos. They soon found a second rifle of a higher calibre beneath the strata of junk that had accumulated there. This one was smeared with filth that closer examination by the light of their torches revealed to be dried blood.

If they weren't spooked before, the Bureau boys were now officially worried. Beside the rifle lay a white plastic bucket, surrounded by a pool of blood that was seeping out to stain everything it touched. It contained something brown and bulbous. It took one brave man giving it a prod with the barrel of his revolver for it to unfurl enough to become identifiable. A liver. It was a liver, carved out of somebody and left here like it was trash. It was only when they tried to slam the door shut in revulsion that the bloody handprints that had been hidden in amongst the rest of the dirt became clear to see.

Something bad was going on here. Not just fish poaching or petty crimes, but something seriously disturbing. Both men had their guns drawn now, fingers on the triggers and eyes darting around the dark.

That was when the screaming started.

At first, it could have been mistaken for the call of an animal. After all, no human being would scream like that. But as it dragged on and on, growing more and more guttural, it became clear that somebody was out there being tortured. Suffering through the kind of distress that would make a normal man drop dead on the spot. Without pausing to think of their safety or the horrors that they were going to find out there by the water, both men took off at a sprint. This evil had to be stopped. The victim had to be saved. The risk to them meant nothing in the face of not just their duty, but their morality.

The shriek warbled on and on as they ran, but as they broke out onto the beach proper, silence fell just as abruptly as the shrieking had started. Now in the silence, with only the thunder of their hearts and the ragged sound of their breath, the Bureau men realised how lethal a mistake they had just made rushing in. In the mist and the darkness, anything could be waiting for them.

Whatever had been making that anguished sound had been all that was on their minds, but the cause of the suffering, the torturer, was out there somewhere, too. They found each other in the dark and pressed their backs together so that they couldn't be ambushed. If this was a trap, then they had fallen right into it. Silence clung to them like a leaden weight, and they did all they could to still their breathing so that they could strain to listen for any sign of trouble about to descend on them.

Still, there was nothing but the lapping of water on the shore. They were just about to relax when it started all over again. So close now that it made both men jump and spin to aim their weapons in the direction of the deafening screams. With a fearful look to one another, they proceeded, creeping inch by inch towards the source of the overwhelming sound. A breeze cut across the lake, bringing a chill to the air but also clearing away the mist that still clung to the silvery sands.

A man became visible, standing with his arms stretched out as wide as he could spread them, head thrown back like a baying wolf. He was the one screaming and roaring and making all manner of inhuman sounds. There was no sign of anyone else around him. Just this man, black in the moonlight.

Coming closer, the black on his skin became more clearly something that he had smeared all over himself rather than the tone of his skin. With a torch turned in his direction, it flicked from black to a dull red. Blood. He was naked, screaming at the top of his lungs, and coated in blood from the top of his head to the tips of his toes. Both policemen were still running scared, but one of them darted forward while his partner covered him to check their victim for wounds. None were apparent.

The man screamed and screamed. His eyes bulging out of his head, the blood trickling down into his mouth to draw out those strange, strangled, gargling sounds that had made the policemen mistake his voice for some animal's call. 'Sir! Sir! Stop. You're safe now.'

The man did not stop. But now his eyes locked onto the policemen, and his screeching tapered down into bellowed words. 'Safe? Not safe. Isn't over. It isn't ever over. Ever since the 1940s, they've been going on. Thirty years! They're still out there. They're doing this to me. They poisoned me. My heart. They poisoned my heart.'

Taking an arm each, the policemen began the slow drag back to the parked vehicles. Blood smeared off onto their hands and their uniforms, tacky and vile, back to black now that their torches had been turned away to the path once more. The man dangling like a rag doll between them was a sack of bones. Either one of them could have carried him like a baby if they'd been willing. Neither of them was.

With his hyperventilating all the way, it seemed only a matter of time before another bout of howling would startup, so they asked him questions on the way, trying to do whatever they could to forestall the deafening racket.

'Who are you?' earned them no response. Nor did any request for information beyond that. They ended up getting his name from the driving license in his glovebox, once they'd excavated enough rubbish out of the way.

They almost had him to their car when the most pressing question came, unbidden, to one of the Bureau boys' lips. 'Whose blood is this?'

That snapped Richard out of his silence as he started to wail. 'It is my blood. It is leaking out of me. The UFOs did something to my skin and now blood is leaking out of me.'

Both cops met each other's gaze and sighed. It was going to be a long night.

The House of Pain

It was a balmy summer's day in Santa Clara County when Anthony Richard Trenton Chase was born. His mother Beatrice had arrived early at the county hospital, the very moment that her contractions started up, but nobody begrudged a first-time mother a little hand-holding. Particularly when it was so obvious that her husband wasn't going to be providing her with any sort of comfort. Richard Chase soon-to-be-Senior seemed to be more frustrated with proceedings than anything else. He wasn't showing any of the usual jitters of a new father – he wasn't butting in or doting on his wife. Instead, he sat at a distance from her, barely even looking in her direction, like he'd rather be anywhere else than by her side during this trying time.

The midwives did their best to make up for the lack of care from Beatrice's husband, but the woman did not make it easy. She was on the verge of hysterics throughout her labour, convinced that something had gone terribly wrong. When the medical staff couldn't find any sign of trouble, she lambasted them at the top of her lungs until she was eventually wheeled into a private room and abandoned there to wait out the long hours of her first labour alone. While the husband had been on the receiving end of plenty of dirty looks when he'd first arrived, now that he was parked outside her room, listening to her scream and wallow in her own misery, a sense of understanding filled the medical staff. If she was like this all the time, then it was hardly surprising that her husband was tired of her shenanigans.

As much as he might have been exhausted with his wife's behaviour, the man sat vigil all through the night of May 22, right through until morning when his son was finally ready to come out into the world. Orderlies had to hold Beatrice down to stop her clawing at the baby's head as it emerged, completely lost to all rationality and obsessed with her impending death by childbirth. A death that never came. Pinned to the bed and bucking in agony, she cursed Richard for doing this to her. Shrieking at the top of her lungs about his filthy sexual appetites and how he had shot his poison inside her. It didn't seem possible that the man could look any more miserable than he already did, yet somehow Richard Senior managed it. He sat there, face glowing red, as the staff of the hospital ran by as fast as they could, stifling their laughter. Many women may have quietly cursed their husbands during labour, but this woman was explicit.

When her work was done and Beatrice had entirely exhausted herself with hysterics, Richard was the one left holding the baby, both figuratively and literally. He awkwardly cradled the mewling little bundle, uncomfortable in the extreme but with nobody else he could pass this duty on to.

Back at the one-bedroom apartment that they shared, things did not get easier for either one of little Ritchie's parents. The hysteria that had characterised Beatrice's hospital stay was not an outlying phenomenon. She was just as emotional and aggressive in her everyday life, driving her husband to the edge of his sanity more than once. Domestic abuse was not a term that was well known in 1950. But even by the standards of the time, Richard's attempts to control his wife's more extravagant outbursts were considered brutal. He was desperately trying to enforce order on a family that seemed to thrive on dysfunction, and when his words wouldn't do the job for him, he resorted to his fists more often than not.

Some women might have quailed in the face of violence, but not Beatrice. She was so riddled with anxiety at the best of times that the danger of real pain didn't even seem to register in her mind. More than just failing to accommodate her husband's demands, she actively needled him at every opportunity, levelling all manner of vile accusations at him if he was so much as a minute late home from work. Infidelity seemed to be the chief among her concerns, followed by drug abuse and poisoning her.

Ritchie was a disappointment from the moment that he was out of swaddling – the subject of constant criticism from his father and crushing oppressive interest from his mother. He was allowed no time to himself, instead spending every waking moment in his mother's company and subject to the whims of her varying moods. Sometimes that meant that he would be treated to ice cream for lunch, sometimes that meant helping her pour all the cleaning products in the house down the drain because she believed that her husband had poisoned them. With nobody else to turn to in the world, Ritchie became the receptacle for all of his mother's many woes. She poured all of her madness and loathing into him, and it didn't take long before her worldview began to twist his.

His father would come home to the pair of them begging to be taken to the hospital because Beatrice had convinced Ritchie that he was sick. He would be woken in the dead of night by his wife fussing endlessly over Ritchie wetting the little cot bed they'd set up for him. Hitting Bea had never done any good – she was too crazy to save from herself – but the boy could still learn. He could still turn out like a normal person if they just put the work in.

Ritchie even showed his father that he could respond to discipline correctly, switching from his mewling mother's self-indulgent drivel to the correct and respectful tone as soon as his father started demanding it. From there, it seemed like the course towards decency was a straight line. Richard Senior would apply the necessary discipline to all parts of his son's life until he was eventually shaped into the kind of man that could bear the Chase name without bringing shame to it.

Shockingly enough, applying even more pressure to a developmentally stunted boy who was constantly suffering the ill effects of one domineering parent did nothing to help his mental state. He became quiet and insular, even for a child with no friends.

When Beatrice fell pregnant for the second time, it coincided with a new work opportunity for Richard Senior. It was a minor miracle that the relationship survived Ritchie's early years, let alone that his parents had remained close enough to produce a second child by 1954. They had been living in a crowded apartment for as long as their son had been around, but with a second child on the way, the necessity of more space was becoming increasingly apparent. Richard also saw this as a fresh start for the family. If he could get Ritchie outside, playing away from his mother's watchful eye, then the boy might get a grip on reality.

The family relocated to Sacramento amidst a whirlwind of chaos. As usual, Bea was at the eye of the storm. As much as she had spent the past four years loudly complaining about the humdrum life that Richard had condemned her to, change was even more terrifying. The routine that she destroyed on a daily basis with her antics was still a solid foundation for her to swing back to in her more lucid moments. Without the same apartment, the same neighbours, and the same town to fall back on, she felt untethered. Her own body seemed to have abandoned her in this time of need, stretching and distorting as she rapidly gained a baby bump, and she lost the romantic attentions of her husband, who she became even more convinced was having an affair when he wasn't attracted to her.

Bea was ever the extrovert. Whatever she felt on the inside was sure to explode out before too long. This new uncertainty played out in the form of abuse. She lashed out, not only at her husband, as usual, but also at little Ritchie, screaming at him for the slightest of offences, then damning Richard for his harsh treatment of the boy in her next breath.

Their new home was a house, the first one that the three of them had ever lived in. It was also on the periphery of suburbia, with easy access to the woods outside of town where Richard planned on taking his son for long hikes at the weekends to keep him out of his mother's reach. Throughout it all, Ritchie had suffered in silence as both of his stressed parents lashed out at him, and by the time that they arrived in Sacramento, it seemed like he would never speak again.

Any loud noise made him flinch. The sound of his parents bellowing made him curl up on himself like a dying leaf. Try as he might to resist the urge, he couldn't control his response to screaming and shouting. It seemed to shut down not only his body, but all of his higher reasoning too. Now that he had a separate room from his parents that he could flee to, the first slammed door or raised voice was enough to send him scampering to it.

When Pamela was born in 1954, it marked a real turning point for the Chase family. Richard Senior saw the opportunity to raise a child properly without infection by Bea's madness. The new baby was the apple of his eye, and he was sure to install a strict set of rules about her care – rules that Bea was surprisingly willing to follow.

Whatever their troubles, the two of them still seemed to care for each other, so now that Richard had put in all the effort of restarting their life afresh, Bea committed to it wholeheartedly. This was an opportunity for her to cast aside the shadow of her anxieties and become the woman that she had always wanted to be. She kept their new house pristine. She kept a smile on her face when she saw her husband. She put in the work that she had been neglecting all of the years they'd been living in the tiny apartment to make things better for all of them. Having a bedroom without a child in it helped in that regard.

As for Ritchie, he was free from the malign influence of his parents for the first time. While the adults fussed over the baby day and night, he was left to his own devices, exploring the garden, the neighbourhood, and the woods in blissful silence.

He attended school where he was well thought of by his teachers and showed around average intelligence for his age, complemented nicely by his extremely pliant, people-pleasing attitude. He didn't seem to know how to respond to praise, so it was kept to a minimum to avoid embarrassment for all parties involved. He made many acquaintances but didn't seem to socialise with any of them outside of class. Even though many children from his elementary school lived in the same neighbourhood, he never sought them out to join him on his expeditions into the woods.

Even at home, his troubles seemed to be receding. The bed-wetting that had always been a source of so much shame seemed to dry up almost as soon as he gained the freedom to roam. School gave his life some structure, and his parents' new pattern of ignoring him in favour of the baby gave him some freedom to pursue his own interests. At last, he had the opportunity to grow as a person into the man that he would someday become.

Cats started to disappear in the neighbourhood. There was no real explanation for it, though some folks blamed wild dogs and cautioned against allowing children free rein to roam alone. Ritchie ignored all those warnings, and his mother's hands were full trying to maintain her façade of normalcy at all times. He seemed to slip her mind.

Of course, by the time he was ten, neither one of them was concerned about wild animals killing cats. By then, his mother had caught him carrying one of the dead cats around the back garden of the house, looking for somewhere to hide it until morning when he could play again. She had taken the corpse and buried it in a flower box, pushing any worries out of her mind beyond the immediate demands for Richard to clean himself up. She could not cope with the implications of his actions, so she assumed he had made some innocent mistake instead of considering that he might be a monster.

Yet her actions remained consistent with somebody who knew that the dying cats were the work of her son, and she took care to conceal the details of it from her husband and the neighbours.

Bea clung to her sanity only by the finest of threads at the best of times, and the weight of this secret seemed to be too much for her to bear. Her old habits began to creep back in – as did her suspicions about her husband. There was no way that he could be as happy as he seemed to be, not when he was with her. He loathed her. She was sure of it. So, if he was happy, it had to be because he was running around behind her back. She was stuck in the house with the wicked children while he got to escape every single day. It only made sense that he was using that time to pleasure himself in every evil way he could conceive of. Where else would the evil in Ritchie have come from if not from his poisoned seed?

With the accusations, so came the recriminations. The more that Bea ranted and raved, the more violently Richard responded, the worse the whole situation got. Eventually, it reached the point where Bea was dressing up the baby the moment that he left for work and wheeling the pram down to spy on Richard. It didn't take long for his employers to take notice of the deranged woman lurking around the office and demand that Richard take his wife in hand.

Exhausted after so many late nights of arguing, and past the point of knowing how to deal with Bea's increasingly erratic behaviour, Richard finally turned to the medical establishment for help.

Mental illness was considered a truly shameful thing in the 1950s, so it was a sign of how bad things had gotten that Richard was willing to drag his family through the scrutiny that seeking psychiatric help for his wife would entail. Bea was resistant to attending the doctor's, having to be tricked into it the first time and lying incessantly to them throughout her treatment to convince them that she was an abused wife of a cruel man who had driven her to despair rather than acknowledging any part of her own responsibility in the matter. It was only when she started spinning tales about how terrible and evil that her children were that the illusion began to shatter and her habitual deceptions were exposed. There was no way that the poor little boy who the psychiatrists had seen flinching away from his mother in fear could possibly have done any of the terrible things that he was being accused of.

Once the initial round of talk therapy had run its course with no noticeable change in Bea's behaviour, Richard was forced to drive her out of town for her next appointments with a specialist in women's issues. This second psychiatrist, forewarned by his colleague's notes on the patient, had a little more success with Bea, helping to bring her more extravagant behaviour back under her control and forcing her to internalize her paranoia and delusions instead of inflicting them on those around her.

Back at home, Ritchie's freedom had continued to expand in her absence. He spent almost all of his time outdoors now, something that his father took as a good sign that he was growing up into a more mature manly man. Dogs started to go missing from the neighbourhood as well as cats, lured out of their gardens by some unknown force. It was obvious now that wild animals were not at work, but something more sinister. Yet even as the missing dogs began to be noticed, their disappearances tapered off again, along with the missing cats. Out in the woods, Ritchie had learned how to hunt. He caught rabbits with his bare hands, staking out their burrows and leaping on them from downwind. He climbed trees and snatched birds from their nests. Even leaping and catching some in mid-flight. The ones that died from the initial shock were lucky. If they survived until Richard pulled his pocket knife out of his pocket, then their future was very grim indeed. He did not deliberately kill any of the animals that he captured, yet every one of them died before he was done with them. Torture wasn't the right term for the things that he did, either, because that implied that the shrieking agony that he caused those animals was the purpose of his actions. In truth, he was exploring them, and through them, himself. In his home life, Ritchie had no control over anything. In school, he went with the flow quietly and did his best to please other people. But out here in the woods, he had his only opportunity to live as himself, to control everything around him like a little god. While his fingers were sinking into the warm flesh of the animals he had brought to the ground, he was their master. They lived or died at his whim. They opened up or were crushed into oblivion as and when he decided to make them. The lack of censure from his parents was assumed to mean approval, so he began bringing his prey back to his garden to toy with in comfort. Yet despite his sadistic behaviour, he remained desperate enough for their approval that he followed his mother's example, burying each of his dead playthings when he was done with them. Often his mother would stand by the kitchen window, watching him doing his dirty work and saying nothing so long as everything was properly covered up afterwards. The perfect microcosm of dysfunction in 1950s America: as long as everything looked pristine, the rotting things beneath the surface could be ignored.

At school, teachers began to notice Ritchie's introversion becoming more pronounced. He spoke only when spoken to, daydreamed constantly, and seemed to be falling in with a bad crowd, following around older children who were smoking during his recess time. He would fall asleep in class, and sometimes there was a smell hanging around him that seemed almost alcoholic, though no teacher dared to accuse a ten-year-old of coming to school drunk.

As it turned out, his passion was not for tobacco so much as it was for fire. From the smoking children, he had acquired matches which he sat and played with so often that he often had soot-blackened fingers. Even in class, teachers had to confiscate books of matches from the boy. Once he had realised how easy they were to come by for pocket change, he would panhandle and hoard them. He had a collection of matchbooks in his bedroom, hidden under his mattress where his mother's cleaning wouldn't find them, and he had a second stash out in the woods, where he would build little fires and integrate them into his sadistic play. The fires ended up being an outlet all of their own for his aggression. As he stared into the flames, he could feel the weight draining out of his body, the rage that he carried around with him everywhere like he was Atlas with the world on his shoulders lessened when the fires burned. It was enough to make him feel almost at peace for a while.

He needed those moments of peace because the situation at home was becoming more chaotic by the minute. His mother's mask of sanity was slipping out of place once more and, rather than coming home to spend even more time being lambasted by his darling wife, Richard was working overtime – something that he more or less was forced to do without thanks or reward to keep a hold on his position after Beatrice had jeopardised it with her behaviour.

As a part of that sanity slip, Beatrice started talking openly with the neighbourhood wives about her horrible life and how badly abused she was by her husband, even going so far as to point out a flower bed and talk about how her son had buried a cat there. While the last point raised some concerns given the spate of missing animals a few years back, it was the stories of her husband's violent nature that really caused trouble for the Chase family. Just as Richard had been beginning to rebuild his reputation at work, these fresh rumours of his terrible home life came to light, bringing condemnation from all corners and embarrassment to the company. It cost him the job that they had relocated to Sacramento for and put a roadblock in the way of his career that he would never recover from. He didn't struggle to find a new job after he had been laid off, but the work that he could get was unskilled labour that paid only a fraction of the amount that he had been bringing home before. Their savings began to drain, and with financial instability came ever more erratic behaviour from Beatrice. It was a vicious cycle that showed no sign of slowing, and the worse Bea became, the harder it was going to be to drag the family back from the precipice. Every workplace that had heard the rumours about his brutality or insane wife but were still willing to offer him a job, were not the kind that he cared to work for. Their fighting, which had abated since moving to the new house, now returned with the kind of fury that gave credence to all of the terrible rumours.

Ritchie couldn't stand it. Outside of school hours, he stayed in the woods or lingered in the garden, as far from the house as he could. Even his usual hobbies of mutilation and arson weren't sufficient to keep him on an even keel. Then to make matters worse, even the peaceful solitude of the garden where he had always been able to escape was interrupted.

One of the neighbours had a radio in his garage that he liked to listen to while working on his car. To hear over the sound of the mechanical work, the volume had to be kept high. It wasn't enough to bother the people in their houses, set away from the road and each other, but for Ritchie, it was a constant bombardment of sound. This was the place that he came to when he wanted to escape the noise of other people, and even that was being taken away from him by this thoughtless neighbour.

Rage had always been a thing that Ritchie turned inward. Even when he was ripping apart living animals with his bare hands, he wasn't doing it because he was angry at them, and it did nothing to reduce the well-stoked flames of wrath that the years of ill-treatment had instilled in him.

Even now, he acted less out of rage and more out of some instinct of self-preservation – lashing out at the only source of suffering that he felt like he could control. He had his matches as always, and there was enough paint stripper lying around the outside of the garage to serve as a plentiful accelerant.

With his work done, Ritchie returned to his garden to sit back and observe the blaze as it grew. What started as a rosy glow on the far side of the fence soon grew into the same kind of bonfire that Ritchie built out in the woods all the time. As the crackling of flames built up, it seemed like it was all that he could hear. The noise of the radio was drowned out. The noise of the screaming and fighting too. All that was left was Ritchie and the purity of the flame.

Sadly, that peace could not last either. The neighbour realised that something was awry and emerged in a panic, shouting his head off before finally realising that the hose attached to the side of the building had not yet been consumed. It was a simple enough matter to put out the fire, and an even simpler matter to identify the would-be arsonist. Ritchie was just sitting there watching the fire with a big grin on his face, after all.

The neighbour dragged Ritchie by the ear to his front door and hammered on the wood with his fist. For the first time that Ritchie could remember, it was his father who rushed to open the door, not his well-trained mother. The sudden noise must have brought out the protective instincts that Richard often insisted were part and parcel of his natural role as the man of the house. Here was his son on the doorstep, being manhandled by somebody outside of the family. If there were any truth to his alpha male posturing, then Richard should have knocked the man on his ass for so much as touching his son. Instead, his already red face darkened further. 'What did you do?'

Ritchie was passed from one set of rough hands to another, and while the neighbour might have felt some reluctance about doing him harm, his father didn't share his compunctions. Instead of protecting him and standing up for him, his father caught him a backhand to the cheek that sent him sprawling, then turned to hear the full story of the fire that his boy had set.

Every time Ritchie picked himself up again and tried to tell his side of the story, he received another slap. If he could just explain that it was the neighbour's fault for playing his music so loud, then surely his father would understand. Surely, he'd take the side of his own flesh and blood. All these years, as his father beat, humiliated, and tormented Ritchie, he had been told that it was all for his own good. That it was to toughen him up and make him ready for the real world that he'd explore once his father was no longer around to protect him, but now that lie was being exposed for its blatant falsehood. All that he had suffered had been for nothing.

Richard Senior apologised to his neighbour and offered to pay for any damages, as this was the only socially acceptable response, despite the fact that whatever claim was made, it would obliterate whatever was left of their savings. After the neighbour left, mollified by the apologies and the offer, Richard turned his full unbridled fury onto his son. Ritchie no longer caught haphazard slaps around his head that set his world ringing. Instead, he had brief glimpses of his father's fists before the world exploded into darkness and pain. The blows rained down long past the point where any sane man would have stopped. Long past the point of corporal punishment and well down the road into attempted murder. In between the bouts of darkness, all Ritchie could see was his father's face twisted in hate. All he could hear was the litany of ways that he had ruined everything and destroyed his family. He was the ruin of them all. He was a monster. He was evil. Yet he was not the one beating a little boy bloody.

He woke up the next afternoon in his own bed, a mess of aches and pains, his eyes puffed up and swollen with bruising, blood trickling from one of his ears. It was the worst beating that he'd ever received from his father, and when he went mewling to his mother's side, expecting sympathy from her – if only because it painted her as the heroine and his father as the monster – he discovered that she had a black eye, too, earned when she had tried to pull Richard away before he killed their only son. There would be no sympathy from his mother and no comfort anywhere. Though he was too stiff to walk any distance, Ritchie headed for the woods. He didn't want to be home when his father came back from work.

Instability

The family finances were already in tatters before Ritchie's little arson attempt, and the repairs to the neighbour's garage were enough to destroy what little was left of their savings. They had been living beyond their means ever since Richard had lost his job, and now the time for pretence was over. They held a yard sale to get shot of as much of their furniture as they could – there wouldn't be room for it where they were going.

The apartment that they managed to rent was just as small as the one where Ritchie had spent his first three years of life. One bedroom, few modern comforts. Yet while Ritchie had been a toddler in the last apartment, now he was a gangly boy well on his way to his teens, and his little sister seemed to take up just as much room as he did or more with all the racket she made. The problems that they could ignore when they had space to breathe were now all pressed up together like sardines in a can. There was no avoiding them, there was no ignoring them. For Ritchie, it was even worse than for the others. He had always craved solitude and silence, and now neither one was an option. The woods where he had spent so much of his youth exploring the world and himself were now denied to him, a car's journey or a day's walk away from the urban sprawl where they had landed in the middle of Sacramento. With the loss of the woods, Ritchie also lost the outlets that he had used to manage his internal strife. There was nowhere in the city that he could stalk and kill animals in peace. There was nowhere that he could build his fires. His parents were ashamed to have lost some social standing. Ritchie had lost his whole world. He was left without any way to moderate his own rapidly fluctuating moods at the same time that he was being put under even more pressure to be perfect at all times.

In the midst of all this, he made the transition to Mira Loma High School, separated from all the friends of his youth by the family's relocation to a different part of town and faced with a whole new world of subjects and teachers with whom he'd had no opportunity to spend years building good relations. Yet despite all of the pressure, Ritchie – or Rick as he was known by his new friends – managed to put forward a good impression. Just as his family had always projected normalcy outwards to the rest of society, somehow Rick managed to do the same. His teachers considered him to be well behaved, if not brilliant, and the other students liked him. Because he kept so much to himself, he had an air of mystery about him that seemed particularly attractive to the girls that he encountered. If it weren't for his reluctance, he could have been quite the Lothario.

Halfway into the school year, his home life imploded in the most predictable of ways. His parents, who had spent their entire adult lives loathing one another, were separating with the intention to divorce. The biggest thing preventing the separation before was societal pressure to appear perfect and a stubborn refusal to admit defeat. Now the pressure had been alleviated by their new destitution. Leaving a bankrupt husband was a lot less of an admission to a faulty marriage than leaving one who was providing well for the family. The decision became considerably easier, too. Given the choice of plodding on in poverty with a man that she hated or moving into poverty and risking raising her kids alone, Bea finally found leaving to be the more appealing option.

One day, Rick was at school as normal. The next day, he was gone. His friends worried about him, and his teachers were confused. It was only after the police made a home visit that the truth came out. Rick and Pamela had gone to live with their grandmother in Los Angeles, entirely free from their father's oppressive presence for the first time in their lives.

Richard had been a harsh taskmaster for all three of the other family members, and after their initial dismay, the children had expected this sojourn with relatives to be a time of rest and relaxation now that they were finally out from under his iron fist. Despite all of his cruelty, they had underestimated just how much of a calming effect their father had on Beatrice. All of her concerns about their health multiplied now that they were away from their father, and it was hard not to let her worries prey on their minds.

Rick seemed to suffer from this considerably more than the more sensible Pamela. He would lie awake at night, trying to feel for any of the symptoms that his mother had insisted that he was showing throughout the day. A common thread was her insistence that he had some sort of bony growth that he would then spend hours poking and prodding at until it was painful, and he felt certain it was something cancerous. Inevitably, this growth would turn out to be mirrored on the other side of his body, and a perfectly normal part of his anatomy. More concerning than those oddities were his worries about poisoning. His mother had spent years accusing Richard of putting chemicals into things around the house to cause her headaches and bouts of perfectly normal illnesses, and now that they were apart and her health seemed to be improving, it gave this mad idea even more credence. Rick interpreted this new 'evidence' of poisoning as proof that his own oddities had been caused by either deliberate or accidental exposure. Every night as he lay on his grandmother's love seat trying desperately to fall asleep before his anxiety consumed him, his fingers would find their way up to his ears, slipping inside and plugging them so that he could listen to the fearful hammering of his own heart. He was certain that sometimes it was falling silent. He was certain that it was skipping beats. Something was wrong with his heart. He was sure of it. His father had accidentally poisoned him, and now he was going to die.

It was only when his mother spent a whole day laid out with a migraine that Rick realised that her symptoms were not a result of poisoning but of some fundamental fault in her constitution. All of these years he had been blaming his father for her illness and supporting her delusions of victimhood. It gave them both pause to wonder.

Beatrice and Richard began exchanging letters after that, and the children got to watch in horror as they courted one another all over again – convincing themselves that all of the problems in their relationship had been fixed by the epiphany of their brief period of separation and that things would go back to the dream that they had promised each other their lives would be when they first married.

It was a lie, of course. Neither one of them could change who they were, what they wanted out of life or, ultimately, their relationship to each other. The damage had already been done and the hatred that had built up on both sides could not be forgotten. All that was left to do now was pretend for a little while before slipping back into the same destructive patterns that they'd always followed.

For Rick, it was a strange time. On the one hand, he was back to his old school routine, surrounded by people that seemed to genuinely care about him. On the other hand, he was back under the roof of his father, a man who had spent his entire life promising that his cruelty was an expression of his care. Another lie, but one that was a foundation of Rick's psyche. A foundation that was now starting to crumble under the weight of reality.

The only positive side to being home again was that his mother's more eccentric behaviour was curbed, and his own burgeoning hypochondria was brought under control by a healthy dose of his father's doubt.

While his faith in the lies that he had built his life on began to falter, so too did his faith in all the other institutions in his life. His teachers found him less eager and engaged, almost as if he no longer cared about his grades. They marked it down as pressures in his tumultuous home life affecting his concentration rather than any sort of aversion to authority, but it was harder to wish away his newfound penchant for lying at every opportunity. It was like truth had lost all meaning to Richard, and the answer that he selected was based entirely on either what he thought his teachers wanted to hear or whatever he thought would be the most amusing to say. The once clean-cut and strait-laced Rick now started to develop a reputation as a rebel, a reputation that did him no favours with the adults in his life but proved a huge boost to his standing among his peers.

His social life began to develop more positively now that he was deliberately spending more time away from home and he had no isolation to withdraw to. While most of the teens had their own peer groups that they clung to religiously, Rick moved freely and found himself welcome among all of them. All doors were open to him. He could sit down at any table in the cafeteria and be embroiled in a conversation within moments.

From this freedom and widespread popularity, Rick soon encountered a different kind of girl from the ones that he'd met before – ones who were less socially upstanding citizens and more fun. Popularity with girls had always come easily to him, but now his hormones were flowing, and with these 'bad girls' who didn't give a damn about their bad reputations, he could suddenly see the appeal of dating.

What followed was a string of short-term relationships that followed exactly the same path. All of the girls that dated him and people that admired him liked the honesty of Rick. They were not authority figures, so he felt no need to deceive them. He never manipulated them or asked anything of people that they weren't willing to give. His romantic forays would build up gradually over time and tended to end amicably when he realised that the girl he was dating had no interest in progressing to a physical relationship. There were no recriminations, there was no rumour spreading, there was just a parting of ways because they wanted different things. The counter culture was finding its feet in the 1960s, and the rebellious aspect of 'free love' was definitely a part of the appeal for young people. It was to these ideals that Rick seemed to cleave, and his increasingly dishevelled appearance and the increasing time that he spent hanging around the 'acid heads' at school seemed to prove that he was just a burgeoning hippy.

Of all the girls that he dated over the first few years of high school, only two were enticed enough by Rick's charms to cast aside the thoroughly ingrained fear of pre-marital sex and stay with him past the point where he started pawing at them. The pattern of both of those relationships proved to be the same as all his others. He would progress as far as he was allowed, then end things when he found that he was not satisfied.

When the time came for them to actually go through with the act itself, his whole plan fell apart. Everything went perfectly until everyone was out of their clothes. Rick was understandably excited in every way except for the one that mattered at that moment. He was able to start having sex, but he couldn't maintain an erection for long enough to carry it through to completion. He broke off each of the relationships soon after a few attempts at sex failed. Sex was his only goal in the relationships, and he had been entirely honest about that. Now that it was no longer possible, he parted ways amicably with the girls, thanking them for their time together and apologising for his failings. He seemed to be completely devoid of any shame about the experience but he was consumed by internal turmoil.

It made no sense that he couldn't get an erection. It had never been a problem for him before. Every time that he had an animal pinned out in the woods and was tearing into its flesh, he was so hard it started to hurt. When he was burning things, he could reach an orgasm without even touching himself. How could it be that in those completely random situations, he was able to maintain, yet when he had a beautiful naked girl spread out beneath him, he was suddenly incapable? It weighed on his mind, day and night. Did this mean that there was something wrong with him? Was this some sign of a new sickness taking root? Even in the dark of his fold-out cot at night, as he tried to ignore the snoring of his parents and sister, he couldn't get himself hard. His sex drive seemed to have been diverted somehow. He still had the need. He could still feel the aggravation and the pressure building inside himself, but now there was no way for him to deal with it.

All of the releases that he had once been able to achieve out in the woods by himself, both sexual and psychological, had now been taken away from him. Those two separate overwhelming forces in his young mind had tangled with each other and been bound up in the sadistic rituals that he had once performed.

Without those rituals, he had to find some other way of letting off the pressure. He could not afford for his behaviour to become too erratic or confrontational while he lived under his father's roof, not if he intended to survive to adulthood. Something had to be done to quiet the urges that were raging inside of him, so, like many before him when confronted with turmoil in their soul, Rick turned to drink.

While there had been odd occasions in the past where he got access to liquor, he now became a devotee, spending all of his hard-earned allowance on booze when he could and shoplifting when he could not. Neighbours in the apartment building soon discovered bottles disappearing from their homes while the rest of the place seemed untouched. In those days, it was still common practice to leave doors unlocked, and Rick was happy to walk through any door he found unlocked and take the thing that he craved.

At about the same time Rick began drinking seriously, the family managed to upgrade their living situation to a marginally larger apartment. He found the opportunity to be alone for the first time since his childhood to be a complex emotional mix. On the one hand, he was able to find a much-needed break from constantly masquerading as a normal human being; on the other, the more time that he was alone, the more time he had to dwell on his own thoughts – thoughts that were turning in ever more macabre and bizarre directions.

When alcohol proved to be insufficient to curb those thoughts, he began to experiment with drugs for the first time. He had ready access to marijuana through the counter-culture social circles that he already navigated, and he became a heavy user in record time. His room, once kept perfectly tidy, and his appearance, once kept perfectly spotless, both fell to the wayside as he delved more and more deeply into these fresh addictions. Through his current friends, he was able to find addicts who were dabbling in LSD, and through them, he gained access to that psychotropic drug. Of all of his drug habits, the LSD use was both the most constructive in the short term and destructive to his wellbeing over time.

Through LSD use, he felt like he was able to explore his mind and confront some of his inner demons. Without the almost shamanic journeys that he took with LSD, his mental state would likely have been considerably worse as his fears about his health and erectile dysfunction consumed him, but the drugs also served to sever his connection to the real world once and for all.

His hold on reality was tenuous at the best of times, and the combination of marijuana and LSD seemed to amplify that effect. There have been numerous studies showing a connection between the use of both drugs and the onset of schizophrenia, exacerbating whatever existing instability exists within an individual, and Rick was no exception.

As his appearance and behaviour deteriorated, his mother continued to be wilfully oblivious to the changes in her son. It didn't matter if his hair was longer than she'd like, or he was staying out late, or he was spending time with the down-and-outs – those were all normal things that teenagers were doing in 1965. She wasn't worried. Why would she be worried? Her boy was perfect, they were all perfect, they were living a perfect life.

Rick was eventually picked up by the police during one of his rambles through town and arrested for possession of marijuana in the kind of quantities that would normally make the police assume that they had apprehended a dealer. Sadly, it was, in fact, just the quantity that Rick regularly consumed between visits to his dealer.

In court, the last of Rick's faith in his father was destroyed. After so long, he had almost forgotten the humiliation that he'd suffered the last time that he expected Richard to stand up for him, but this time there could be no doubt or confusion. This was not a man being misled by a neighbour or confused about his son's actions. Richard actively chose not to hire a lawyer to defend his son, and he chose not to show up at court to support him. Richard had seen his name dragged through the dirt enough in Sacramento without being associated with this kind of behaviour. It was bad enough that stories about his 'crazy wife' still did the rounds every few months.

For his crimes, the juvenile court sentenced Rick to community service. From that point forward, his weekends belonged to the city of Sacramento, and he would spend them picking up litter, scrubbing off graffiti, and generally undoing all of the mess that his friends made throughout the week. Only in the evenings did he find his time unoccupied and unsupervised.

If his drinking and drug use had been out of control before, now it peaked. His father now made a point of ransacking his room on a regular basis to hunt for any drugs or paraphernalia, so the only time that he had access to marijuana or liquor was outside of the household.

At a house party one Saturday night, Rick drank so much that he lost the ability to speak, then went tearing off down the street screaming incoherently. Fearing that it would bring attention to their illicit drinking, one of his closest friends was deployed to retrieve him, or at least to put him to bed somewhere that he wasn't going to cause trouble. What followed should have been a tense chase through the streets of Sacramento, if it weren't for the fact that his friend had also been drinking, and as a result was finding Rick's staggering and gibbering to be absolutely hilarious. The chase could have been ended several times over if the friend hadn't been doubled over with laughter at the sight of him.

Eventually, Rick was brought down and hauled off to a friend's bedroom to sleep it off. Yet even after his ability to speak in English returned, his talkative mood persisted. It was a wonder to the friend who'd never known Rick to share anything about himself willingly, and they sat up until the early hours of the morning chatting. His virginal friend pressed him throughout the night for stories about his sexual adventures, hoping to live vicariously through Rick's numerous experiences with the ladies. Instead of the raunchy tales he was expecting, he got an earful of Rick's erectile dysfunction, with the other boy talking at great length about how it was affecting him and ruining his life.

By the time that the two of them had awoken the next day with reeking hangovers, a mutual agreement seemed to have been reached to never speak of such things ever again. Both boys feigned alcohol-induced amnesia. But even though it would never be acknowledged, just speaking out loud about his problems seemed to have released a little of the pressure from Rick. While he knew that he could never talk to friends or family about his 'little problem', he now had the confidence to approach a doctor to discuss it. All that he was lacking was the opportunity. Anything he said to the family doctor, who was a friend of his father, would inevitably be relayed, and as a minor, a hospital visit was out of the question. He had to wait it out until he was away from his family's influence.

The years rolled by with the ongoing upturn in the family finances serving to ease the arguments. The same patterns from before the separation had come back in force, but with more breathing room in the larger apartment, the conflicts did not become confrontations so easily. Instead, all parties had somewhere to retreat to, for them to think over what had been said and done and for their loathing to grow and fester. Even the fights had been a release of sorts. Now the family lived out their days in a pressure cooker, just waiting for the inevitable explosion that would end it all.

At school, Rick's defiance of authority and lack of ambition led to his grades declining further, and without the excuse of his parents' impending divorce, the teachers began to take their frustration with his lack of effort out on him. Complaints were sent home, and Rick would return to school the next day battered, bruised, and no more inclined to obey than he had been the day before. If anything, each beating just seemed to make him more resistant. Where other boys would break, it just seemed to harden his resolve.

He continued to self-medicate with alcohol and drugs when he could, but his father had cut him off financially in the wake of his declining grades, so he was forced to steal what he needed instead of purchasing it illegally. In 1966, he was caught in the apartment of one of his neighbours, stealing a bottle of whiskey, and once again, his father let the police get involved with no effort to shield his son from the consequences of his foolish actions. This time he got a slap on the wrist and a warning rather than an extension to his community service sentence, but it put all of the neighbours on guard and destroyed his reputation locally. No longer was he the teenager with troubles – now he had graduated to being a juvenile criminal in the eyes of Sacramento.

When High School came to an end, he graduated with mixed grades ranging from a few C's and D's to a hefty clump of F's. Academia had once been the place where he could excel, far from his family's malign influence, but now it had become nothing more than the latest humiliating failure in a long litany of them.

The weight of his parents' demands now began to fall more fully on Rick's shoulders. In his father's eyes, he was a man now and should start acting like it, finding a job, supporting himself and getting the hell out of their house. Meanwhile, his mother continued to pursue her own idealised version of her son, the obedient boy who'd scored so well when he first started school. She wanted him to go into higher education and make something of himself.

Of the two potential futures, Rick couldn't help but feel like the one in which he was painted as a genius with boundless potential was the more appealing of the two. Not to mention the prospective freedom that higher education could offer him in comparison to locking himself into the strict schedule of a job that he hated, like dear old dad.

Rick took an introductory course at American River College to see where it might lead him, and there found the first opportunity to live a little bit of life, not as his father's son or his mother's fantasy, but as himself. Within a few weeks of arrival on campus, he availed himself of the health services and found himself passed into the care of a psychiatrist specialising in adolescent problems to discuss his erectile dysfunction. He talked at great length about his sexual failings, carefully skirting around any mention of sadism or fires – he had learned his lesson well enough about those subjects in his early life that he now kept those parts hidden from everyone; yet even without that puzzle piece, the psychiatrist was quick to point out that repressed anger was often the cause of male impotence when there was no obvious physical cause. Rick unburdened himself of all the stories of his family's problems and the impending divorce that he predicted for his parents. Finally, he began to let slip some details about his emotional instability before the conversation skirted too close to the subject of how he had managed these pressures in his childhood and he shut down entirely.

There had been more than a few red flags thrown up during the consultation that made the psychiatrist suspect that there was some more pronounced mental illness at work within Chase. Schizophrenia was known to come on in the teenage years and to be exacerbated by the marijuana that Rick had entered the office reeking of. Parts of Rick's stories seemed to blend fact and fiction, reality and fantasy in a way that was not consistent with a stable worldview, and it seemed possible that this was a symptom of a problem with his ability to perceive the world as it was rather than just a blurring caused by the stress that the boy was under.

The patient already seemed twitchy and anxious to leave after saying too much, and the psychiatrist wanted to use a gentle touch so that Rick didn't cut off his treatment entirely. There wasn't enough to build a case for institutionalisation in the notes, so the only way that the two of them would remain in contact was if Rick willingly came back. As such, the doctor tried to teach him some simple coping methods and gave him a brief lecture on his anger. The particular kind of erectile dysfunction that was plaguing Rick often came out of feelings of hatred and anger towards women, usually caused by problems with their mother. As such, he recommended that Rick try to spend some time with his mother and repair that relationship. It was not what Rick wanted to hear, but he took the advice stoically before leaving, never to return.

He did not speak to his mother. He did not spend more time with her. Even as damaged as he was, he could recognise the further warping that spending time with her caused him. His burgeoning hypochondria had not only continued to grow throughout the years, but it was now at the point where he was constantly attempting to monitor his own heartbeat, touching himself all over in public when he suspected that there was something out of place and making nonsensical queries to the college health centre on almost a daily basis. While he did not outwardly display all the same signs as his mother, having learned to hide them from his father or risk his wrath, that did not mean that he was not constantly in fear for his health and life.

Into this mixture of chaos that was Rick's life, another element was now added. His parents separated once more. While they had flown apart in a rage previously, now the situation was different. They came to a mutual arrangement to part ways rather than continue to plague each other's every waking moment. His father would still contribute some portion of his wages to Beatrice for her upkeep, and the children were free to live with either one of them as they chose. Pamela chose her father without a second thought for how it would make her mother feel, but the more sensitive Rick felt pinned between the two crumbling pillars of his mental landscape. He did all that he could to spend time with both of them, technically living with his mother, but visiting his father every other day. Neither parent had moved far from their original apartment, within easy busing distance of one another, and there was little effort required to make the trips. Both of his parents became truly appreciative of Rick for the efforts that he made during that time, finally recognising that his sensitivity was not a sign of weakness but kindness. All of this time, his father had been trying to beat the softness out of the boy when in fact it was his softness that he should have been appreciating the most. The boy was a source of great comfort in those days, having more heart-to-heart talks with his father than Richard Senior had managed with his own old man in his entire life.

Suddenly Richard was confronted with the uncomfortable truth that he had misused his son badly through the years, and despite it all, Rick was still willing to turn the other cheek and offer his father and tormentor nothing but kindness in return. While Beatrice had initially felt the sting of betrayal doubly when she first saw Rick slinking off to spend time with his father when that man already had Pamela to keep him company, she soon recognised this strain of kindness in him too, and could find no fault in him for it. She had always done her best to treat her son with kindness, to counterbalance his father's cruelty, but now that they were alone, she found that she had nothing to give. The only thing that could be said in her favour during the marriage was that she was a better parent than the man actively beating her child, and now, without that comparison to make her look better, all of her shortcomings were on display.

Rick treated her with compassion, and she lashed out. It would be easy to blame her mental illness for the cruelty that she treated him with, but ultimately, he was treated like her emotional punching bag because she knew he'd take it, the same way he had been taking it his entire life. Beneath the grandeur of her delusions of persecution and sickness, she was as much a bully as his father had ever been. She was just subtle enough about it that Richard didn't understand what was happening. When children are abused by their parents, they do not stop loving the parents, they stop loving themselves. Richard turned all of his justified anger at his life inward, assuming responsibility for it all. He was the one at fault. He was the one who had ruined everything.

Even watching her son crumble before her eyes did nothing to curb Beatrice's torment. The lines between her sickness, her rage, and her son blurred. His hypochondria was elevated by every day that they spent together, and his rage spiked each day they were apart, when he got some sense of just how bizarre her behaviour was in context. Richard Senior could see how Beatrice was tormenting the boy, correctly assuming that it was in much the same way that she had troubled him through their years of marriage, but while he had the mental fortitude to withstand it and the emotional intelligence to recognise what was being done to him, his son had no protections.

Worse yet, Richard Senior had been placed in a position where anything that he said could be dismissed as bitterness towards his wife. Now that he had learned the error of his ways and was trying to right his relationship with his son, he was confronted with an impossible situation: He could sit back and watch Beatrice harm the boy or intervene by voicing concern regarding the acts of cruelty at the potential cost of damaging the tentative relationship he had been working so hard to build with Rick. In the end, he did what he had done throughout the whole marriage. He kept his mouth shut and waited.

The Poisoned Mind

It would not take long before Rick was pushed beyond the point of no return by his mother. She manipulated him expertly into spending less time with his father, using the same pseudo-medical rhetoric that fuelled her own madness to justify his isolation from his father. Poisoning was discussed in great detail, and the same spurious evidence that she'd presented over and over was rolled out again without anyone around to provide the usual counterbalance of sanity. After spending an extended amount of time at her home, the 'symptoms' that he had been trying to ignore for his entire life became increasingly pronounced, and she was able to convince him that they were a result of his father's ongoing attempts to poison him. She pushed and pushed at Richard, demanding that he choose between the two of them – the parent who had loved him and cared for him all his life or the man who had beaten him once a week since he was old enough to talk back. The woman who had given him life with her own frail body, or the man who was trying to take that life from him by poisoning him.

Rick stopped eating during his final visits to his father's house, then remembering all his mother's talk about poisoned soap dishes when he was younger, he stopped bathing, too. When his health still seemed to be declining, he started to suspect that the food and cleaning supplies in his mother's home had also been contaminated, so he stopped using those, too.

His grades at college plummeted as his ability to concentrate on anything outside of his own head was destroyed. He dropped out soon afterwards. His dishevelled and filthy appearance put a halt to his social life, and the job that he had managed to hold down for almost three months fired him for his inability to function as much as the embarrassment that he was bringing to them. All of the tethers that had been holding him to reality were being severed one by one, leaving only Rick and his sickness behind.

He felt weak all of the time – in no small part due to his very real starvation – but instead of looking for answers in his actions, he began to believe in the lies that his hypochondria was whispering in his mind. His limbs had lost their strength, he was exhausted all of the time, clumsy and useless like he had forgotten how to move around like a normal person. It could mean only one thing – his blood was being pumped too weakly around his body to provide it with the energy it needed, and there could be only one cause of that. His heart was shrinking. Every day he got a little bit weaker, so his heart was getting smaller. Nothing else made sense. Eventually, it would shrink so small that he wouldn't even be able to get himself out of bed. Then he'd just end up lying there waiting for it to shrink and shrink until it vanished completely, and then he would be dead. Dead forever of a vanished heart. He had to stop it. He had to do something to make the shrinking stop. His shrinking heart explained everything that was wrong in his life. It was why he couldn't love people properly – he didn't have enough heart. It was why his dick wouldn't get hard – there wasn't enough blood getting pumped into it. Everything in his life could be explained away by this one grandiose theory, but what could be causing it?

At first, he had accepted his mother's theory of poisoning at face value, but now there was no way he could be consuming more poison. Not without soap or food or anything to drink but water straight from the tap. The poison had to be getting into his system somehow. His heart was definitely still shrinking. Even his vision seemed to be dimming now as there wasn't enough blood to keep his eyes working right.

As soon as he worked out the vector for poisoning, he'd get better. He'd be able to eat and drink and wash and do all his normal things the moment that he worked it out, but there was nobody else around that could be doing this to him. He began reading extensively about the UFO phenomenon, about the effects of radiation and pseudo-science fiction about death rays. He started to ponder just what kind of poisoning he was suffering from – if it was some evil-looking green liquid being poured into him like in the cartoons, or if it could be something even more insidious.

Every morning, he stood in front of the bathroom mirror, examining himself for the tell-tale marks of different poisons, searching his skin for stick-marks where someone had injected him with a toxin, staring into his own eyes, with his own ever-dimming vision, to see if he could still make out blood pumping in the tiny veins around their edges. The latest in the long line of symptoms, along with the usual hammering of his heart, was the shortness of breath that he felt when he was thinking about his sickness – a tightness around his chest that had to be a heart attack. Cold sweats. Tremors.

He worked himself into a frenzy, trying to explain away the obvious with increasingly convoluted reasoning until finally, he realised that the simplest explanation was the correct one. All of his life, his heart had been shrinking because of poisoning. Therefore, the one who had been poisoning him all his life had to have been there his whole life. The only one who had always been there, everywhere that he went and even now, was Beatrice.

It was so obvious now that he could see it. His mother had put this sickness in him. She was the one obsessed with health. The one who revelled in getting attention when he was ill. She was even the only one who seemed to know that he was being poisoned at all. All of this time, she had been acting like she was worried about him when she was gloating over his stupidity. She was killing him. All of his life, she had been killing him, and he'd been too blinded by his love of her to notice.

Just as soon as he came to this realisation and started screaming, there she was bursting through the bathroom door in a panic of her own. His mother, his killer. Teaching him to trust nobody but her and poisoning him all the while. Teaching him to hate himself so much that he would just lie down and take it when she decided it was time for this game to end and for him to die.

He wasn't going to let her.

Strength flooded back into his arms as fury took him, and he tackled her into the door frame. His numb fingers closed around her neck, and he bore her down to the floor, still shrieking at the top of his lungs. He was not going to let her kill him. He was not going to stay here and let her poison him. He was going to live.

Her face turned red, then purple. Tears poured down her cheeks and just as suddenly as the revelation had struck him, so too did sanity re-assert itself. He unlocked his hands from around her neck and scurried away until his back hit the sink. She was his mother. She loved him. She'd never do anything to hurt him. Not poisoned soap. Not tainted food. Not a thread and a bottle of poison trickling in his ear while he slept. That was madness. Whatever was wrong with him, he had been born with it. That was why he'd started fires, killed animals, wet the bed, become impotent, withered down to this wretched husk of a man – not poisoned by some external source but poisoned by his own faulty nature.

He crawled back to his mother, weeping and begging forgiveness, but it was too late. She saw the monster that she had created now. For all her fear of imaginary dangers, when this one was looking her right in the face with snot running down his lips to bubble up in his sobs, she could recognise it all too clearly. The moment that she could draw a breath through her crushed throat, Rick was sent to his room to pack up his things. It wasn't safe for him to be around her anymore. That much was clear.

Calls and arrangements were made, and Richard Senior came over to collect his son's things. He would be swapping places with Pamela for a while until he found his feet.

As it turned out, he found them rapidly. Once he was out of the house and away from his mother, he was able to eat and bathe again, restoring at least some of his strength. His sanity seemed to creep in a little more slowly. He was still twitchy and obsessive about his health throughout his stay with Richard Senior, but Rick became more and more like the boy that he had once been with every passing day. Before a week was out, he was able to function well enough in society to start helping out a little around the apartment, cleaning not only himself but the living space, too. Trying to encourage this sort of progress, Richard Senior began leaving his son a shopping list and some money every day so that he could bring in groceries and try to get back to normal interactions with others.

It was just the push that he needed to get out of the house and out of his head. At the local store, he bumped into old friends from school and found that he was able to hold a conversation, just like he used to. Through the grapevine, he even found a room for himself in a house on Annandale Lane with a couple of girls that he had been friendly with all through his teenage years. It was perfect.

Though it was earlier than he had expected, Richard Senior was delighted to find his son ready to start moving on with his life, and while he wasn't certain about the moral implications of the boy living with two girls, he was willing to let it pass if it meant that Rick was out from under his roof and taking steps toward a life of his own.

Being Normal

Everything was provided to Rick by his father. His share of the rent was paid up in full, furniture for his new room was acquired at no small cost, and a healthy allowance was allotted to him to live off each month. All that he had to do was take care of himself and establish something like a normal life – two things that he had proven himself entirely incapable of many times over.

It was February of 1971 when Rick moved out of his dad's apartment, and it would take only a few months before his new living arrangements had completely fallen apart. The girls whom he had befriended in high school were not accustomed to his new behaviour, expecting the quiet and charming Rick that they had known back in his halcyon days. Instead, the ragged-looking wretch who slunk around their apartment reminded them more of a rambling homeless man. Rick would speak to himself frequently, but rarely in any sort of understandable language. Rather, he seemed to make whining, keening sounds in his throat that seemed more like animal noises than real attempts at communication. He would become non-responsive for hours at a time, just lying around staring sullenly up at the ceiling. The girls had heard rumours about Rick's drug use, but the seventies were rolling in, and the general opinion on drugs was that they were 'far out' and that anyone who was not comfortable with their regular use was some sort of bootlicker trying to pander to authority. For this reason, the girls were accepting of many of Rick's eccentricities as they made every attempt to stay 'hip' with the social in-group.

If his problems had been limited to his various drug addictions, then it is likely that he would have been able to maintain his place in the home without any issue, but sadly there was considerably more going on beneath his greasy hair than the bubbling of various narcotics. Instead, his odd behaviour began to draw notice. Talking to himself and twitching was fine when they were alone, but when they had company around, he made things awkward. He refused to wash himself, so his aroma somehow permeated the whole house, necessitating keeping the windows open all the time, regardless of the weather.

Time seemed to have no meaning to Rick. He'd come and go at all hours, sleeping through the day and banging around his room at night. The rumours that he'd lost his mind after high school, and that was why he had disappeared, laid heavily on the minds of his new roommates. They began to really worry about the man that they had invited to live in their home. Not for his wellbeing, but for their own.

One evening, when the girls brought a couple of friends home from college, they hoped to find that their lurking housemate was out roaming again. When they got to the living room and found it devoid of his usual presence and stench, they were elated. Perhaps this wasn't going to be the horrible embarrassment of an evening that they had anticipated.

They managed to maintain that hope all the way through the first round of drinks, and it was only when they returned from the kitchen to find Rick standing in the middle of the living room chatting with their guests that their illusions were shattered. Rick was naked. The reason for the lack of smell was that he'd managed to shower himself that day before flopping back down into his bed naked. When he'd heard voices in the other room, he'd initially ignored them, assuming that they were just another of the many whispers and sounds that he heard every day that logic could not explain. But when the voices were raised in laughter, he realised that joy was not a part of that usual litany, so he came out of his room.

Whether he was aware that he was naked and just didn't care, or he had forgotten his state of dress in his detachment from everyday reality was unclear, but his roommates and their guests were too mortified to say anything, sitting in miserable silence until he became bored of talking to himself and wandered back to his room to settle in for the evening.

Attempts to talk to him about his behaviour later were hopeless. He didn't recall the incident in question, and even if he had, there was plenty of crossover between the hippy and naturist movements that he could use to justify himself during lucid periods.

The lucid days were almost more disturbing for those around him than those that he spent stoned out of his mind and gibbering away to himself. It was in those moments that the true cruelty of his mental illness became apparent. When he was a wreck, it was easy to just discount him as a nuisance, but when his reality and the one that everyone else inhabited intersected, he managed to be as charismatic and surprisingly intelligent as he had ever been. It reminded his housemates that he was an actual person, one who was clearly suffering in the hold of some truly horrific personal demons.

In the weeks that followed his exposure to the girls and their guests, they took all efforts to isolate him from the rest of their social life to avoid the awful questions about him, but when they came under pressure for having such a big house to live in and never using it for parties, they crumbled almost immediately.

The next Saturday night that came along, the house on Annandale Lane was heaving with visitors. As usual, Rick seemed to be oblivious to everything that was going on around him, staying secluded in his room until the party was in full swing. When he realised that there were drugs and drink being passed around, he mysteriously came back down to earth and started to mingle, almost like a normal person.

As the evening wore on, his mask of normalcy began to slip. He lost the ability to hold a coherent conversation, much like many of the other heavy drinkers, but he continued rambling nonetheless. Eventually, he was found face down on the floor of the living room, still rambling away to himself. The only time he made any attempt to communicate was when a couple of good Samaritans tried to hoist him off the shag rug. Then he screamed until he was left alone.

From then on, his roommates abandoned any hope of having a normal social life as long as Rick lived in the house with them. They threw no parties, and everyone politely sidestepped the idea in conversation – just one encounter with their nightmare roommate had been enough to dissuade anyone from coming around again.

Throughout this time period, Richard was not a happy young man. While he had lived with one of his parents, he was constantly under observation, and his wilder behaviour was kept in check by social pressure. Now that he lived alone, there was nobody to tell him no. Nobody to stop him from following his train of thought right off the end of the line into an explosive crash. At first, he revelled in his newfound freedom, drinking and abusing whatever drugs he could lay his hands on to excess. He received a bank deposit from his father every month, and he would burn through it rapidly, indulging all of his vices. He began to hoard magazines and books in his room on a variety of esoteric subjects, obsessing over the possibilities of the many conspiracy theories that were springing from the mind of the counter culture. The lost continent of Atlantis. The Hollow Earth. Alien abductions. Secret experiments. Nazi holdovers in South America. Endless medical textbooks that he had no understanding of, yet pored over as though the knowledge might pass into his brain through osmosis, just by being close to them. All of his obsessions came to the fore now that nobody was telling him to stop, and if they had remained fixations and no more, then it wouldn't have been a problem, but for a mind with so poor a connection to reality, every one of the bizarre stories that he read seemed equally plausible. Why wouldn't the moon be a hollow Nazi UFO base? It didn't seem any less likely to him than any of the other strange things that he saw on a daily basis.

The fundamental force that had always driven Rick was fear. He had been born afraid and screaming, and every day on from that first one, his parents had worked tirelessly to fill him with dread. The threat of physical violence seemed all too real to the survivor of a decade of domestic abuse. The threat of someone poisoning the water supply seemed even more plausible to a boy who'd spent his whole childhood hearing his mother fretting over the same possibilities. In Rick's world, anything was possible, and that was a terrifying prospect.

He had to protect himself. He had to find some way to diffuse his anxiety. The drugs had proved a useful distraction over the last few years, but now they just seemed to send him into a downward spiral of obsession and terror. He needed something real and palpable that he could hold up like a talisman against all the dangers of the world. Luckily he was an American, and he had been provided with the perfect model of behaviour for when a man was frightened but could not admit weakness. He went out and bought his very first gun.

His weapon of choice was a .22-calibre pistol that he took to carrying with him everywhere, tucked into his waistline. It was a security blanket for him. A reminder that he was prepared to face all the myriad dangers of the world. That he was not just a helpless victim on the tides of fate. If the enemy came for him, then he could defend himself. If he found out that somebody was trying to get him, he could get them first.

He began to sleep in the closet at night with the gun balanced on his lap. There was only one way into the closet, and he would have a much better chance of defending himself if somebody came at him head-on. Even this solid tactic wasn't enough to ease his fear. He had to be sure that nobody could come in silently, so he took a hammer, nails, and a board of wood in with him and sealed the door shut with some awkward hammering.

Yet still, his paranoia wouldn't quiet. He heard whispers behind him in the dark of the closet. Plotting and planning his demise. He lasted only a few nights in there before he realised that there was some sort of secret passage leading into his room through the closet. This must have been how they were getting to him while he was sleeping to administer the poison. No wonder he was waking up aching after sleeping bundled up in a tangle of limbs in the cupboard; he was giving them free access to inject him full of their experimental chemicals.

The next morning, his roommates were woken early by the sound of hammering. Rick was boarding his closet shut. It barely even raised an eyebrow at this stage, compared to some of his behaviour – a bit of DIY was practically normal.

In the days that followed, he would board up his window and use the temporary board that he had once used on the inside of his closet on the door to his room. This ever more insular behaviour was almost a relief to his roommates. If he was boarded up in his room, he wasn't out in the common area scaring them or their guests. When a long silence descended, they relaxed enough to invite friends around to visit once again – hoping that Rick had finally sunk into some sort of routine and wouldn't trouble them anymore.

Once again, the sound of people and drinks being passed around was sufficient to draw Rick out, but this time he seemed more like his old self. The twitching wretch that had scurried past them in silence over the past week had been subsumed back into his sociable personality. He was still dirty and bedraggled, but he was also the charming old Rick that everyone missed from their school days.

He drank, but not to excess, and the girls he roomed with were stunned to see him turn down a joint. Maybe this new silence was genuinely a sign that he had turned things around for himself. If anything, he seemed to be even more gregarious than he used to be, laughing and chatting with everyone at the party, even the strangers that he would previously have been wary of. Instead of sapping the joy out of the room, all of the energy that he usually turned inward seemed to be pouring out of Rick. There was a tidal flow as he moved around the apartment, the heart of the party wherever he was. It was only when some of the guests had to leave for the night that things took a turn for the strange.

Rick drew another smattering of laughter when he hung out the window, shouting mock threats at the departing guests, 'Yeah, you'd better run!'

If that had been the end of the joke, things would have been fine, but Rick never knew how to do anything halfway, and that was why everyone found him so hilarious. He whipped the pistol out of his belt and waved it at the guests outside, who went from amused to horrified in a moment as he pointed it at them. Inside, the tone of the party shifted. He had gone from a fun-loving guy with a manic edge to a wild man with a gun in the eyes of the partiers in an instant. He tucked the gun away again, but even though it was out of sight, everyone still knew that it was there. An awkward silence descended, and the party fell apart soon after. It was only then that Rick's roommates knew for certain just how dangerous and precarious their situation was.

The next day, they staged a house meeting, demanding that Rick move out. They told him plainly that his behaviour at the party and in the months before had frightened them, and they didn't want to deal with it anymore. They needed him to find somewhere else to live.

For Rick, this was a slap in the face. He had been painfully aware of what a disappointment he was to his friends and had been doing all that he could to reverse the flow of their resentment. With every complaint he'd received, he had adjusted his behaviour to correct, and still, he was told it wasn't enough. No matter what he did. It was never enough. They wanted him to be quiet, so he was quiet. They wanted him to stay away from their friends, so he did. They wanted him to be the social butterfly that he had been in high school, so he came out of his shell and lavished his undivided attention on their guests. And this was how they repaid him for his efforts?

Confrontation was not in his nature. His father had beaten any hint of it out of him at an early age, making him into the easygoing boy that everyone had liked, so he didn't even attempt to express any of the anger that he was feeling in that moment. Instead, he did what he had always done when confronted with a situation he found untenable – he withdrew. He went back to his room, boarded the door shut and ignored all of their attempts to talk to him.

The girls formed a house meeting not long after. They were genuinely scared of confronting Rick, given how unstable he had become and the fact that he was carrying a gun around with him at all times. That same fear was what made them want him gone, but if he was unwilling to move out, then they had no choice but to leave themselves. There was student housing available to them on campus, so they were able to go whenever they pleased. The landlord would come to Rick for the rent every month since he was still there, so it wouldn't do the girls' reputations any harm. By May of 1971, just three months after he'd moved in, he was left completely alone in the house.

If his mental health had been deteriorating before, now it plummeted in a free fall. There was nobody around to see what he was doing, to check that he was alright, or even to check if he was alive. The drug use that he had curbed to try and ease his roommates' fears now came back fully, and his hypochondria kicked into overdrive, with every sensation now interpreted as a symptom of some dreadful underlying condition. All attempts to care for himself faltered and failed as his paranoia about toxins being slipped into his food crept back in. By the end of the month when the landlord contacted his father, he was a bag of bones – terrified of everything and everyone outside the confines of his room. It took Richard Senior and the landlord working together to break down his barricades and winkle him out of his hiding place.

Rick was returned to his father's home, where he rapidly pulled himself back together. His skeletal appearance began to fill out once more, and he seemed to become lucid within a day of eating food for every meal instead of his previous diet of liquor and drugs.

Being alone had left Rick empty, and his madness had spread out to fill that void. Having seen what sitting idle did to his son, Richard set out to fill every waking moment with activity. It was a conundrum for the older man to find work around his perfectly ordered house for the boy, so instead, he commissioned him to undertake some DIY tasks. He had been handy enough with a hammer and nails in his apartment, so Richard figured the boy could manage a little more woodwork. Fixing a table leg that was too long. Rebuilding a kitchen cabinet. Simple tasks with simple instructions that nonetheless would strengthen Rick's confidence in his skills and lead him on to greater things.

In his childhood, if Rick had not performed perfectly, then he was punished, but this new, softer version of his father just wanted him to try, and in the face of that new kindness, Rick's sense of ambition seemed to rekindle. His mind turned toward those projects instead of to the chattering voices at the edge of his perception. While his father did not demand that he improve each day, Rick began to expect more of himself without prompting, growing frustrated with each failure and elated with each success. By the end of a few weeks in his father's care, all of the promise and potential that he'd shown as a young boy seemed to come flooding back. He was working at the level of a journeyman joiner and could have gone and found work with any of the firms in town without much effort. Even Richard Senior was impressed with how far the boy had come so quickly, and he was ready with his praise.

He told his son that he was proud of his work, that he was proud of his progress, and that he could go out and find work anywhere in the world with skills like his. Any expectation that he'd had that the boy would be pleased to hear this evaporated the moment those last words left his lips. The tentative smile that had been creeping onto his son's face was wiped away in an instant. He didn't want to get a job.

At first, Richard was taken aback by that announcement. How could he have gone so wrong with this boy that he didn't even want to be a contributing member of society? It was shameful. Seeing the impending disapproval on his father's face, Rick was quick to clarify. He'd been sick for a long time, and he was still building up his strength. He'd be happy to do work like this for the family, where his fallibility would be easily forgiven, but he wasn't ready to put his stamina to the test in a real working environment. He didn't believe that he was well enough for that yet.

It was indisputable that the boy still looked like a wreck. Even after he'd been bathed and fed up to the best of Richard's ability, Rick still looked like something you'd find washed up on the beach. Now that his more erratic behaviour had been curbed again, he looked very much like somebody to be pitied, and that was the trap that his father fell into time and time again. Richard Senior was consumed with guilt over his part in the creation of this mess of a human being, so now he did whatever he could to please Rick and make him well out of some belated attempt at redeeming himself.

Rick took advantage of his father's guilt as much as someone with no real desires or ambitions in life could. He took as much comfort as he could find in his father's home and tried to work out what he could take with him when it was all over. It was to this end that he approached his father, a month into their cohabitation, with a request. It was the first time that Rick had asked for anything from the man, so his attempts to communicate were a little clumsy.

He wanted a car. It would give him the freedom that he so desperately craved without the permanence and pressure of maintaining his own home. Richard's initial response, after discovering that Rick had somehow found time to get his license in the midst of all his other nonsense, was outright refusal. The boy didn't have anywhere to go, so why would he buy him a car? Rick was sullen at the complete rejection of his idea and began to retreat back into himself. Richard came up with what he thought was a healthy compromise. He'd buy

Rick a car, provided Rick paid for his own petrol by getting a job. The job would even give him somewhere to drive to every day, to make the purchase of the vehicle worthwhile.

Rick was even angrier than before. His father was trying to trick him. Richard had just been biding his time, waiting for Rick to actually want something before snatching it away from him and levelling completely unreasonable demands on his son. Why would Rick want to get a job? There was nothing that he wanted to buy. He had all the money he needed from his father, he had a circle of friends who'd secure whatever new drug he wanted to experiment with, he could even get his meals made for him by heading over to his mother's house. It made no sense to go out working when all those things were taken care of, and he had much more pressing matters on his mind.

Seeing the miserable state that Rick had been reduced to had been the last straw for Richard Senior. His only son had become a gibbering, worthless wreck, and while he had shouldered some portion of responsibility for the state of the boy and was making amends, he could not claim that he was this disaster's sole instigator. Beatrice had made this boy, growing him within her and then strangling his growth with her apron strings and madness. For so long, Richard had turned his anger at the pathetic nature of his son onto little Rick, but now he found himself too invested in helping the boy blossom to continue stamping him to the ground. The anger had to be turned outwards, somewhere, and Beatrice with all of her eccentricities was the perfect outlet.

After dawdling for years, he began pressing to finalise his divorce from Beatrice. Societal expectations had changed since the fifties, and even if they hadn't, nobody could fault him for divorcing a mad woman. All the evidence that he needed to present was the state of his son.

The divorce was another nail in the coffin of Rick's sanity. Throughout all of their troubles, he had always assumed that his parents would eventually resolve their problems and reform the monolith of parenthood that his psyche had leaned on so heavily through the years, but divorce had an entirely different sense of finality to it. He was enraged but had no way to articulate why the situation was making him so angry. Most of the psychological forces at work on Rick's mind were far beyond his understanding. He may have tried to ascribe meaning to them, but it was all based on his limited perception – like a caveman trying to appease a storm.

With no other human contact, he began to argue with his father, lashing out now that there was no more risk of violence in response. Over and over, the two of them found non-issues to fight about, with Rick's favourite being a return to the matter of his demands for a car. Eventually, the patience of Richard Senior reached its end. He could handle being kind to a quiet and withdrawn mess of a man, but extending his kindness to this little bastard who kept leaping on any opportunity to squabble was more than his guilt could force him to endure. He shipped Rick off to live with his mother until their tempers could cool or the boy felt ready to find work and move out for himself. Richard had always been a believer in 'pulling yourself up by your bootstraps', so he was now wondering if he'd shown Rick too much kindness in the recent months, if he'd made things too comfortable for the boy to want to step out on his own.

Things would certainly be different in his mother's house.

The Sickness

When Rick arrived on his mother's doorstep with his one suitcase of belongings, she welcomed him back with open arms. Everything about their parting of ways was forgotten, and she did her best to dote on him as she wished she could have when he was just a little boy. She was free of her tyrannical husband now – they were all free – so she hoped to make up for lost time without his spectre hanging over them. Pamela did not share her mother's enthusiasm. She had no fond memories of Rick, only really knowing him from his teenage years when he began to go off the rails. She was horrified by his cadaverous appearance and bizarre mannerisms. She described him to her friends as 'spooky' and often fled the house to be away from him, spending more and more time in the homes of others and ultimately running away from home entirely on several occasions. Her fear of Rick seemed justified. Between his raging tantrums with no real outlet and his mother actively encouraging his paranoia about his health issues, he was a nightmare to be around, and that wasn't even taking into account all of the other weird and terrifying things that he did as a matter of course. Lying face down on the floor moaning and groaning as dark thought after dark thought chased through his mind. Talking away to himself in a language that only he seemed to understand. Hissing, grunting, squealing, screaming. In context, spooky seemed like the mildest possible term to describe him.

Where his father had always dismissed his health issues, Beatrice took every minor complaint at face value, rushing Rick to the hospital at all hours to be examined by doctors who would, ultimately, find nothing wrong with him. He was treated once for hypertension after his anxiety had worked him into such a fury that his heart rate would not slow. Another time he burst into the emergency room complaining that his stomach had been turned upside down and reconnected wrong. The medical staff found no evidence of any such surgery and suggested politely to his mother that psychiatric evaluation might have been in order. Beatrice felt a fresh kinship with her son in those moments. All of her life, her worries, illnesses, and pains had been dismissed by doctors as nonsense and overactive imagination. She would not see her son slighted in the same way. As erratic and bizarre as Rick's behaviour was, Beatrice seemed intent on matching and supporting it at every stage.

He would rage and rant at the slightest provocation, trying to physically intimidate his mother into giving him what he wanted. His demands for a car were not met with denial this time but instead with a promise that she would start scrimping and saving money for him so that he might have it as soon as possible. Even so, he was furious to be 'denied' yet again. He would argue with anyone about anything, the rage and resentment that he had buried deep inside of himself surging up to the surface in completely unexpected ways, even to him. He would often find himself looming over Pamela or Beatrice with his fists clenched and his face locked in a rictus of fury without remembering why he had been angry a moment before.

Headaches had always been a feature of Rick's daily life – tension headaches as a result of the considerable stresses that his various mental health problems put him under – but now he became convinced that they were symptomatic of something more serious. He heard creaking in his head at night – possibly a hallucination like so many of his others, possibly the tightening of the muscles over his skull – but he interpreted it as the sound of his bones grinding together. His mother immediately jumped on this new complaint, telling him that she thought the bones of his skull had never fused when he was a baby, causing her no end of distress and several hospital visits where nobody would even examine him to determine if she was correct or not. That was all the evidence Rick needed to fuel this latest obsession. He was certain that the bones in his skull were moving around. If he could just catch them moving, then he'd be able to prove it to everyone. He shaved his head in the family bathroom using the tiny blunted razor that he usually used to tidy his facial hair when he remembered. There was a substantial amount of bleeding, which he also interpreted as symptomatic of his condition. After all, if his skull was smooth the way that it was meant to be, why would there be raised parts for the razor to catch? His new look startled both of the women in his life. If he had looked half-dead before, the bald head made him look entirely cadaverous.

He spent hours staring in the mirror, trying to catch the bones in motion, fumbling at his head the rest of the time as though the bones might leap into motion the moment that they weren't being observed. There was a spate of hospital visits to deal with this new crisis, all ending in screaming arguments with doctors who seemed more than a little dubious about Rick's claims after the first time he came in. The intervening visit, when he claimed that somebody had stolen his pulmonary artery, did not help.

His inability to differentiate reality from fantasy, and fantasy from his dreams, increasingly led to these situations. His anxieties and paranoia would play out fully in his dreams, with abduction and vivisection featuring heavily, and his rising the next morning convinced that some part of him had been altered or removed. Beatrice started driving him further afield to find new hospitals to visit when the local emergency rooms started turning them away.

It took only a few months of desperate trying for Beatrice to realise that this living situation wasn't going to work out for anyone. Rick needed to get out of the house and find some way to work through his issues. Preferably somewhere far from home.

She did the unthinkable and gave him a loan of her car and the little cash that she had saved so that he could go on a road trip, supposedly to 'find himself.' It was a kind enough gesture to shock him out of his recursive spiral. He thanked her, he smiled, he acted like he was her son, instead of some monstrous spirit inhabiting the boy's corpse and making it walk around. She was so delighted with his response that she didn't even think to ask him where he was going.

For weeks, Rick vanished without a trace. The silence should have been a comfort to his family after so long suffering through his ranting and screaming, but instead, it felt like the quiet before the storm. Like doom was lurking somewhere, just out of sight. Nobody had bothered to inform Richard Senior that his son was going on a road trip. As far as he knew, the boy was still tucked up safe in his mother's home, driving her mad instead of him. The first thing that he knew about it was when he got home from work to find his phone ringing. It was a penitentiary officer from the state of Utah. Rick had been arrested for driving under the influence while making his sojourn through that state. His mother's car had been impounded, and he had refused to give any of his contact information to the police, instead insisting that nobody would be interested in helping him. He wasn't carrying enough cash to clear his fine, so there was no place for him other than the state prison, where he had been in solitary confinement since very nearly the first day because his bizarre behaviour was making the other inmates fractious.

Richard drove west for twelve hours to sort things out, and a substantial amount of money, in fines and legal fees, had to change hands before Rick was released into his care. The boy looked even worse than when Richard had taken him in after he'd been living alone in the now abandoned house in Annandale Lane. His eyes were sunken, he still reeked of liquor after days in jail and court, and his hair had begun to grow back in, not in the smooth waves that he'd carried atop his head all his life but in ragged patches, jutting out in random directions. They didn't speak throughout the whole journey home, including an overnight stay in a roadside motel. Richard, because he was so bitterly disappointed in his son bringing shame on the family name. Rick, because the idea that his father would call in sick and drive across country to come and rescue him from prison was an entirely alien idea to him.

Every time that he felt like he had a grip on reality, some little detail would change, twisting and distorting the whole image like he was looking through a kaleidoscope.

On his return home to his mother's house, it was clear that his latest misadventure had done nothing to make him more stable. He claimed that he had been gassed while he was in prison. His extraordinary medical conditions continued to be present, but now he attributed them to surgical intervention while he was unconscious in prison, or an aftereffect of the gassing. Confrontations with his mother continued to escalate as he returned to his old pattern of blaming her for his sickness.

Yet despite all of this, he somehow managed to maintain a social life. After bumping into some old friends while he was out roaming, he was invited to a gathering at their apartment. The two men that lived there had a fellow student over for drinks and thought that Rick might make a nice cornerstone for the group. Rick came prepared with his own bottle of liquor wrapped in brown paper. The evening rolled on without much incident. Rick managed to hold up his side of the interaction, and while he'd steer the otherwise normal conversation in bizarre directions sometimes, that was taken as entertaining rather than a worry. When the beer ran out, the two men that lived in the apartment made a quick run to the liquor store to restock, leaving Rick and the girl alone together for the first time. The conversation dried up instantly, but she made the mistake of thinking that it was because of the perfectly normal awkwardness of these situations. It was not.

Rick climbed onto the sofa beside her and grabbed her breasts with both hands. She told him no, but it was as if he couldn't hear her. She had to push him right off the sofa to make his rough kneading stop. The moment he was back on his feet, he came after her again, and what followed was a truly pathetic chase around the apartment. He would come at her, fondling her and trying to get her out of her clothes, and she would wrestle free of him and put some distance between them. Rick didn't seem to get angry at her for denying him, the way some men would. He didn't even seem to be aware that she was talking to him most of the time, like he was somewhere else and his body had been left behind to act out his desires. This horrid little chase continued for nearly a quarter of an hour before the owners of the apartment got back and intervened.

It was only when he was asked to leave that Rick seemed to snap out of his fugue. He started screaming. 'Nobody has the right to tell me where to go! This is America. I'm free to go where I want and do what I want.'

It went on and on for almost an hour, arguing back and forth between the three men while the poor abused girl hid in one of the bedrooms and sobbed. After that first hour, it seemed like he'd relented. He picked up his things and left, slamming the door behind him.

Everyone in the apartment breathed a sigh of relief, but their freedom from Rick was extremely temporary. Two minutes later, he let himself back in and was creeping through to the bedrooms when he got intercepted, and he let out a flustered explanation that he'd left his cigarettes behind. This time, Rick tried brute force rather than just screaming at the top of his lungs. He still yelled, insisting that nobody had the right to make him go anywhere or do anything, pushing one of the men along the hallway, getting closer and closer to the bedrooms where his victim was still curled up on herself in the sheltering arms of one of the roommates.

By this point, they'd all had enough. As aggressive as Rick was, he didn't have the physical mass to stand up to the average man his age. When the fight turned physical, it didn't take long for him to be overpowered. In the scuffle, a .22-calibre pistol fell out of his belt.

The other roommate spotted it on the floor, snatching it up and tossing it into the other bedroom before Rick could notice it was gone. The brawl continued in a one-sided fashion all the way back along the hall to the front door, but try as he might, the owner of the apartment just couldn't force Rick out. By now Rick had mostly degenerated into ranting again, having exhausted his meagre stamina early in the pushing match. 'Call the cops if you want. I don't give a shit. Nobody can tell me what to do. Nobody!'

The police were called in short order, both by the roommates and their scowling neighbours. The deputies hauled Rick away to spend the night in the county jail to await sentencing, but his illegal ownership of a firearm never came up. The guys who'd invited him around already felt bad enough about getting the police involved – they didn't want to make things worse for Rick by showing off his gun.

By the next day, Richard Senior was down at the jail bailing his son out yet again. He hauled the boy back to his mother's house, and for a little while, it felt just like the home that Rick had grown up in. Both of the adults in the room screaming at each other about him at full volume.

The only thing that they seemed able to agree on was that Rick couldn't go on living with his mother like this. His behaviour was getting worse and worse. They needed to get him out of the house and out from under his mother's toxic influence.

In May of 1973, he was shipped off to Los Angeles to stay with his grandmother – the only member of the family that he had not yet alienated or terrified with his bizarre behaviour.

He was on his best behaviour when he first arrived in LA. His grandmother took in his home-cut hair, ill-fitting clothes, and sallow face and decided in an instant that her flighty daughter had been taking care of the boy very poorly indeed. She'd whip him back into shape in no time, but first, he'd need to start pulling his own weight.

His grandmother owned and operated a school for developmentally challenged children, kids that the public school system had utterly failed and whose parents were quite ready to sweep under the rug if possible. Since he had his license, Rick took over from his uncle the job of driving the bus around to collect the students every morning. For the first couple of days, Rick was delighted. He enjoyed driving, and he felt like he was being valued for his skills for the first time. By the third day, it had become routine. He became bored, and when Rick's mind began to wander, it would head into the usual maze of imaginary illnesses. He was late to pick some children up and early to pick up others. Parents complained that he was unclean, with dirty hands and dirty clothes. That he smelled bad. That they shouldn't be making developmentally impaired adults take care of children at all.

Rick barged into the emergency room complaining that his pulmonary artery had been removed. Tests discovered that his blood pressure was through the roof, so he was treated for hypertension, and for a brief moment, he felt like he was being taken seriously. It soon passed. The moment that his uncle came to collect him, he was lambasted for skipping out on work for his hypochondriac nonsense. He was put back to work the next day without even getting a chance to pick up the prescription he'd been provided, losing it sometime in the next week somewhere amidst his usual filthy living space. His work continued to worsen until his grandmother was forced to intervene directly. If he could not work, then he could not live under her roof. She had no time for the lazy or the useless – if he would not carry his weight, then he was heading home. He arrived back on his mother's doorstep less than a month after he'd last graced it. Everything was accelerating. He no longer lurked around the house waiting to feel ill before making complaints over the span of days. Instead, he dramatically claimed to be suffering from cardiac arrests, kidney failure, and all manner of other catastrophic illnesses to force his mother to call out an ambulance for him. They attended once only, during one of his supposed heart attacks, hanging around only long enough to deny him care before moving on to a real call. From then on, Beatrice became his personal chauffeur, taking him to the hospital on an almost daily basis to deal with one complaint or another. Before long, even she was tiring of the same story playing out over and over – she'd drop him off and wait in the car.

In December, he entered American River Hospital in Sacramento and told the attending doctors and nurses that somebody had stolen his pulmonary artery, stopping the flow of his blood. This was obviously untrue, but Rick was showing many signs of illness, so his examination proceeded beyond the cursory. With a captive audience of medical staff, he explained that his skull bones moved around and that his head hurt all the time. This led to a consultation with a physician who specialised in head injuries, who rapidly ruled out any sign of physical damage, instead attributing Rick's erratic behaviour to a 'psychiatric disturbance of major proportions.' Rick would have accepted any diagnosis gladly and clung to it for dear life, any diagnosis except one of mental illness. He fought tooth and nail as he was dragged off to the psychiatric ward, claiming loudly to anyone in earshot that he knew as much about medicine as any five of the people attending him and that they should be listening to him instead of trying to imprison him against his will. Oddly enough, this did not persuade anyone to his side. He was placed in the psychiatric ward for observation, and sometime in the late afternoon, his mother realised that he wasn't coming back and drove herself home to enjoy a nice peaceful evening imagining her own illnesses.

No official diagnosis came out of his stay in the psychiatric ward. After the sedatives failed to calm him on arrival, an extensive blood screening was ordered, turning up near-lethal doses of various recreational substances in his bloodstream. What had been taken for schizophrenia at a first glance could very well have been some sort of toxic shock due to the preponderance of chemicals in his system. This theory seemed to be supported by how rapidly Rick calmed down and began acting normal again just a day into confinement. When his mother was called on to visit him, she saw the change in Rick immediately. He did not want to be imprisoned here, so suddenly he became capable of sublimating all of his bizarre behaviours and acting like a normal person again. He had her convinced that this was all just a big misunderstanding, and with only a little bit of cajoling and manipulation, he had her check him out of the ward and back into her loving care. He didn't manage to get out of the ward without one of the doctors who'd observed him passing along a warning about his drug use, however – a warning that his mother overheard and incorporated into her own delusions about her son. The way that she understood it was simplified, of course, but it was sufficient to shift the blame away from her and her beloved son. The drugs were what had made him go mad, so as long as they could keep him off the drugs, he should go back to being his lovely childhood self again.

This task proved more difficult than anticipated. Unless Rick was observed at all times, he would slink off in search of some method of self-medication, and his mother simply was not up to the task of confronting him each time. For the first time in their relationship, Beatrice and Richard Senior began working together as a team, switching off tasks based on their strengths. Rick was also flung back and forth between their two houses on an almost daily basis as they tried to ensure that he was being watched at all times. The instability did nothing to help his mental state.

After a run of vivid dreams, Rick began to believe that he was the reincarnation of one of the Younger Brothers, who had been members of Jesse James's gang. His language and mannerisms changed while he was adopting this persona, much to the confusion of everyone around him. His temper continued to flare without warning whenever his usual personality reasserted itself, with his mother most often receiving the brunt of his scathing and extremely personal insults.

Throughout it all, his family remained certain he was getting access to drugs somehow, leading them to invade his privacy constantly, searching through his belongings when he was out or sleeping, feeding into his already burgeoning paranoia.

Unknown to his parents, Rick was slipping away sometimes, but he spent considerably less time seeking drugs than he did pursuing the long-lost taste of freedom. He made an application for Social Security assistance and welfare so that he might be able to afford to buy things for himself without parental involvement. To receive the benefits from the state, he had to undergo a physical examination to determine the medical reason that he was unable to work.

Normally, Rick relished a medical observation as both affirmation of his beliefs and a challenge to be overcome, but this time, he was aware that he needed this doctor's support to get what he wanted. His devil-may-care attitude towards reality and the truth was abandoned, and he carefully calculated the responses that he would give, well in advance. The examination was a success, from Rick's perspective. The doctor judged him to be neurotic, but not insane, and observed his physical deterioration as a sure sign that he would not be capable of holding down a job. The application for Social Security support was rubber-stamped and Rick was sent on his way with a new secret source of income.

The possibilities changed for him then. The downward trajectory of his life was suddenly reversed. He started eating again, intent on improving his health. He had no trust for his mother and insisted on cooking his own food to prevent poisoning, but his energy had switched from depressive to manic.

He would press slices of orange against his forehead so that his brain could absorb the vitamins from them. If a milk carton was left open, he would give it a taste test to ensure it hadn't been interfered with and add dish soap before drinking it if he thought that it might have been contaminated. He talked to himself incessantly as though there was someone else there with him, and when questioned, he would suggest that he had been developing his telepathic powers so that he could block certain people from controlling his mind, and he had discovered that there were other psychically sensitive creatures out in the universe that wanted to communicate with him.

After reading an article about cardiac patients, he demanded that his mother purchase an oxygen tent for him to sleep in. Despite her usual desire to indulge his delusions, the apparatus was outside of her price range, and the ensuing argument ended in Rick accusing her of trying to control his mind and poisoning him all of his life and his slapping her to the floor.

The past few months of self-care had made a world of difference to Rick. He had packed on weight, almost all of it muscle, and his personal hygiene had returned to a near acceptable level for society. When he hit her now, it wasn't the haphazard slap that he'd managed in the past – it was enough to knock a tooth loose and leave her unconscious.

Without the sense or the shame to flee the scene of the crime, Rick left his mother lying on the kitchen floor and went on about his day. When he returned home that night, his belongings were packed and his father was waiting alone for him in the house. It was clearly no longer safe for him to live with his mother, so they were going to make another attempt at giving Rick the freedom to control his own time. He was warned in no uncertain terms that using drugs would result in the payments to his landlord being stopped, but with everything he wanted being offered up to him on a silver platter, Rick laughed off the suggestion. His health was finally improving – he wasn't going to risk that by taking some chemicals mixed out of his sight by strangers and criminals. That was the Rick of the past. This Rick planned on surviving and thriving. Whatever the cost.

Run, Rabbit, Run

The new apartment on Cannon Street was a big step down from his parents' places and the house that he'd rented before. Barely more than a single room, it nonetheless would serve Rick's purposes well. He had no car, but his childhood bicycle had been brought along so that he had means of transportation, and, of course, he had a source of income that was completely unknown to his parents, which he could use to continue purchasing books, magazines, and miscellaneous other products for his 'self-improvement' projects.

Now that he was out from under their watchful eye, he rode his bike into town and recovered the pistol that he had left behind when he was last arrested, even going so far as to apologise to the man who'd invited him over with excuses about his mind having been controlled and poisoned. His old friend took this to mean the drugs rather than literal mind control and poison and accepted the apology, happy to be free of the gun that had been sitting like a lead weight in the back of his mind and closet for the years since Rick had dropped it.

While he was never going to be the most fastidious, Rick's little apartment did not degenerate into filth the way that his parents had been expecting. He had stacks of his magazines and nonsense pamphlets everywhere, and his kitchen could do with a good clean, but ultimately, each time they visited to check up on him, the place seemed to be more or less the same.

Rick continued his exercise regime, cycling for miles every day, and now that there was nobody to interfere with his food, he felt considerably more secure in eating proper meals. His anxiety about his health didn't go away, but now he felt like he was actively managing it instead of everything being out of his control.

Just a short distance up the road from his apartment by bike, Rick found a place that would become the focal point of his coming days: A rabbit farm. At first, he spent his time just lingering around, watching the rabbits in their runs, but soon the owners began chatting with him on each visit, and he felt obliged to make a purchase. Every day, he would take a rabbit home with him in a cardboard box punched with holes, and every day he would butcher it alive on his kitchen counters – listening carefully to the song of its dying squeals as if there were some message encoded within it. This was the best food he could be eating. The safest. Freshly killed animals that nobody could have interfered with. He had seen them alive, he had watched them die, and then he had consumed them. It was a pure transaction. He could feel the life energy flowing out into his body to replace all that was being stolen from him after every meal of rabbit. His parents marked the improvement in both his health and his mental state during their visits and felt satisfied that their boy was finally on the road to recovery after so many years of struggle.

In truth, torturing those rabbits to death did make Rick feel better than he had in years. He found that his libido, long-dormant beneath layers of rage, was able to resurface after he started killing again. Death and sexual pleasure were inextricably linked in his mind. With his self-abuse and animal abuse back in full swing, the tension that had marked his descent into madness began to ease off. He attributed it all to the rejuvenating power of his rabbits. If there was just some way for him to make the transferral of life energy from the rabbits into his body purer, then he might be able to go back to living a normal life like everyone else without having to worry about his body crumbling while he wasn't paying attention. He wanted more than just survival now that he had tasted the possibilities. He wanted to live.

It was not difficult for an ex-drug addict to lay his hands on medical supplies, but even once he'd acquired the equipment he needed, Rick wasn't sure how much of the rabbit's blood he would need to inject before he saw results. He had always drained the blood out of the rabbits in the process of prepping them for the roasting tin, but usually he had just discarded it or drunk it. Drawing it up into the syringe was tricky because his hands were shaking. These tremors had become commonplace – a sure sign that his sickness would return if he didn't continue with proactive treatment. He needed the blood. It was the only way he would improve.

He shot a full syringe of rabbit blood into his arm, and almost immediately he could feel himself coming alive. The flow of energy had always been slow and steady when he'd eaten the rabbits, but in his arm, it was almost electric. It spread as fast as his withered heart could pump it around. He felt like he could almost see the new, good blood under his skin, moving along his veins towards his heart where he might finally be healed. He cooked up the rest of the rabbit and ate it with every intention of wringing the very last drop of life out its skinny frame, but this rabbit did not taste the same as the others. He wondered if the tackiness in his mouth and the itchiness were a result of the rabbit blood, if the rabbit tasted wrong now because he had rabbit blood in him and was part rabbit. Did that mean that injecting human blood would make him more human? Would food taste better if he was more human? Would the shaking and the pain fade away if he could consume them and make them a part of himself?

The red mark of the rabbit's blood was still crawling slowly up his arm, so he stripped out of his clothes to watch it rise. He didn't need clothes anyway, not if he was a rabbit. Besides, his skin felt all prickly and hot anyway. Who needed clothes when they were growing rabbit fur on their insides?

It was in that same state, stripped down to his underwear and passed out, that his father found him on the 26th of April, 1976. The boy was delirious and feverish, and with his newly rebuilt body, it took all of Richard Senior's strength to wrestle him into clothes and the car so that they could drive to the hospital. At first, the staff were sceptical about Rick having any legitimate illness, but a cursory examination revealed his high fever. He was strapped down in a bed, and instruments were attached to monitor him until a cause for his current state could be diagnosed. It was around about that moment that Rick regained consciousness and his usual raving began. He took one look at the monitor and started screaming. His blood pressure was zero. It was exactly like he'd always said.

His heart wasn't beating. He was dead. He'd been dead all along. A corpse walking the earth. Controlled by wicked forces in their flying saucers with thought transmitters. His mother was working with them. Making him sick. Keeping him weak. Refusing him oxygen.

In his frenzied state, he nearly tore his way out of the bed. It took his father and a pair of orderlies to pin him down until the initial flood of mania passed and he could be reasoned with. 'The rabbit was bad. It was a bad rabbit.'

His father managed to calm him down further, and they managed to get a little more of the story out of him. 'I ate the rabbit, but there was something wrong with it. It had battery acid in it. It must have drunk battery acid. Or absorbed it. And now it is eating through into my bloodstream. It was the rabbit.'

There was no indication of food poisoning, but the tell-tale marks of septicaemia were on display. Blood poisoning from where he had injected a foreign body into his bloodstream. With the suggestion that it was rabbit's blood, the doctors were able to put together a treatment, and the infection began to recede to the injection site.

It was almost a week before Rick was back to his own version of sanity, and during the long feverish nightmare he'd just lived through, his ranting had turned to topics that he knew better than to discuss in public. The aliens. The Nazi base on the moon. The things that they were controlling him and making him do. The voices that spoke directly into his brain through telepathy. The way that killing was the only way to ease his suffering. It was more than enough to concern the doctors. So, when the time came that he believed he was back to his full strength and he tried to discharge himself, he discovered that he could not. He was considered a danger to himself and others, and the court had ordered his confinement in a mental health ward until the nature of his illness could be identified and treated.

He was taken back to American River Hospital, where he had first been examined for signs of mental illness, and a panel of new tests were conducted over a much longer time. It was decided that the earlier assumption of toxic shock was wishful thinking at best, and that his frankly deranged consumption of drugs and now animal blood were symptoms of the paranoid schizophrenia that he had worked so hard all of his life to mask.

Sadly, the paper-thin mask of sanity that he had been holding up all of this time had been one of the only restraints on his behaviour that was left now that he had lost all faith in his parents' influence.

It was as though a flood gate had opened. He ranted endlessly about his sickness. About his missing arteries. His shrinking heart. The voices that he heard. The secret world that was playing out behind the scenes of our own, unknown to all but the psychically sensitive. The staff at the hospital were concerned enough that when the 14-day hold for assessment was up, they applied immediately for some form of conservatorship over the man.

The court proceedings were brief and swift, with only two brief interruptions by Rick to confirm that he had spoken to a lawyer and to ask what would happen if he was to leave the hospital. He was informed that either the police or hospital staff would return him by force and that he should not attempt to leave without permission.

Two days later, he broke out of the ward in the dead of night during a shift change. For all that his internal world was chaotic, he was not stupid or unaware of the things going on around him – they were merely augmented by his hallucinations and delusions, not obscured.

Assuming that his apartment would be under observation by the police or his invisible enemies, Rick headed for the only person that he thought he could trust to help him: Richard Senior. Twice now, Rick had been in trouble with the law, and twice his father had intervened to save him from the consequences. He had finally earned his son's trust back after the years of abuse, and now it was about to be lost all over again. Rick snuck into the house to find his father was already sitting up waiting for him. The hospital had called as soon as Rick's absence was noticed.

His father gave him the first hug that the two of them had ever shared, and promised him that he'd get him somewhere safe where he couldn't be hurt any more. They got into the car, and Richard Senior started to drive, heading away from the city hospital and out towards the countryside that his son had always loved. It soothed Rick to be out of town and see the trees passing the car by. It calmed the hammering of his heart, and now that he was safe in his father's care, he actually slipped into sleep, lulled by the gentle vibration of the car window's glass against his head.

When his eyes opened again, they were outside some big stately house and dawn had broken. Flowers were growing everywhere, butterflies flitting between them, and trees everywhere beyond the fences. Some serious-looking men in white clothes were outside the car, and panic was about to launch Rick into another wild sprint when his father caught a hold of his arm. 'These people are going to help you get over that bad rabbit. They're going to help you get your strength back. They'll take good care of you.'

It was just enough acknowledgement of his delusions to catch Rick's attention. Nobody had ever listened to him before. Not really. Everyone had dismissed him as a lunatic without believing a word he said, but now the one person who mattered most to him in the world was doing just that. Proving that he believed Rick. Affirming that his trust had been well placed.

The serious-looking men helped Rick out of the car and took him off to a private room where he'd rest until his strength returned. The whole place was pristinely clean and so quiet that Rick felt like he could hear his thoughts for the very first time. The room was small but nicer than his apartment by several degrees. He could be content here while he got back to normal. He should have trusted his father all along. The man always knew what was best for him.

The hospital had been planning to transfer Rick to Beverly Manor for long-term treatment anyway. Psychopharmacology was still in its early stages, and the time that it would take to find the right cocktail of chemicals to silence his screaming mind could stretch into years, so somewhere with better security and a dedicated staff of carers was ideal.

He may have arrived a day early, but it was without the cost of the hospital having to conduct the transfer, and it allowed him to be introduced to the place in a very soothing manner. His breakout had actually proven quite helpful to the medical staff trying to treat him.

The first few days at Beverly Manor, Rick accepted his new lot in life gladly. Throughout the day, he was free to roam the grounds and enjoy the peaceful atmosphere, and while they gave him lots of medicine for his food poisoning, it wasn't like in the hospital when it was being forced into him against his will. They gave him his pills along with his food. He was more concerned about the food than the drugs. He had no idea who prepared the food, or what contaminants they might have slipped in. He certainly wasn't getting any of the life energy that he'd been absorbing from the rabbits in these meals, and he suspected that it was starting to show.

The tremors that had always plagued him were coming back, and while the headaches weren't as constant, he was feeling many different things in his skull instead. Shuddering inside his brain. Long periods of fuzziness, like some fog had rolled in to silence telepathic communication. The strange numb absence of feeling where all of his pain should have been. The orderlies came in to find him lying completely still on the floor, face down, one morning. When they managed to wrestle him up onto the bed, he explained that his whole body had gone completely numb, and he assumed he was dead. His dosage was rapidly adjusted.

The nurses soon started trading shifts with each other to avoid attending on Rick. He talked about blood so often that he acquired the nickname of 'Dracula' among the staff. Something that was only exacerbated by how often he was discovered with blood on his face and no explicable cause.

When the staff engaged with his rambling about blood being all-important and vital to the transfer of life energy between bodies, he soon degenerated into graphic descriptions of how he killed different animals. He explained why rabbits were his favourite. With other animals he felt guilt, but with rabbits, the actual act of breaking them down made things so much easier. Rabbits weren't like living things in his eyes, they were like little machines. When he cut off their skin, they were like a mechanical toy underneath the surface, elastics glued to the solid lengths of bone. A well-designed toy, but a toy nonetheless, and easy for a steady hand and sharp blade to take apart.

Rick would hide parts of his meals around his room for reasons that the staff could not initially parse. In particular, he seemed to like to keep a stockpile of bread. There were plenty of patients who'd suffered from food insecurity in their lives, so it was believed that Rick was just doing the same. Sadly, he was not. The food that he was saving was bait.

The first time that a dead bird was found outside of his bedroom window, it raised no eyebrows. Animals died. The second time, when the body was examined more closely and discovered to have been decapitated, began to raise concerns. Rick lured birds in with scraps and crusts then captured them with his bare hands, twisting their heads off their necks and then drinking their fresh blood right from the source. He had flushed several of their bodies down the toilet but found that the larger birds wouldn't fit, so he had to discard their remains out of the window. In light of these latest developments, two of the nurses that he had been giving close personal attention to during their rounds quit on the spot. They did not feel safe caring for Rick – they did not want to be anywhere near him if they could avoid it.

While he'd been nicknamed Dracula, a more accurate literary parallel for Rick's behaviour was the character of Renfield, from the same book. A character that had encountered the dark horror of a monster beyond his understanding and had responded by trying to apply what he had learned from the experience to his everyday life, consuming living creatures in an attempt to absorb their life-force and extend his own life. It is after this character that the mental illness known as Renfield Syndrome would later be named. Also known in medical circles as 'clinical vampirism', Renfield Syndrome is a picture-perfect match for many of Rick's behaviours and symptoms, right down to anxiety about health and weakness of the blood.

Rumours of his behaviour began to spread throughout Beverly Manor and then beyond. Even back in Sacramento, whispers had started up about what Rick Chase was up to nowadays – whispers that eventually reached the ears of his mother, who had been appointed as his legal guardian and conservator during the court proceedings back in June. She could not stand to have her name or that of her son, dragged through the dirt.

He was checked out of the hospital at his mother's direction on September 29, 1976. His discharge report suggested that his social skills had greatly improved, that he had a realistic view of his personal problems, and that with continued medication, his thinking could remain clear, with his more dangerous behaviours kept under control.

The man that Beatrice collected from the hospital bore little resemblance to the boy that she had once known. This Rick was coherent and calm; he did not twitch or speak to people who were not there. His symptoms may have persisted, but the medication had given him enough breathing space to actually address them as symptoms instead of accepting them as facts. His mother still had a healthy fear of her son after their last time cohabiting and had made arrangements for his Social Security grant to go directly to the landlord of the Watt

Apartment Complex. Groceries and utilities would be coming out of her own pocket, which in turn was being filled by the labour of her ex-husband as a part of their divorce agreement. At no point was Richard Senior informed that his son had been taken out of medical care – because he would have strenuously objected. Beatrice had been granted full power over her son's life anyway, so Richard Senior's approval was not required.

From September of 1976 through to 1977, Rick Chase lived as a normal man. The voices and panic in his head had been quieted, if not silenced, and he was able to move through the world invisibly, without causing anyone harm or providing cause to take notice. He attended bi-weekly medical appointments to check on the long-term effectiveness of his medication. He reported no additional problems with his health. It seemed like he would be able to begin the long slow crawl back up to living like everyone else.

That was when Beatrice decided that he didn't need his medication any more. To her mind, drugs had always been Rick's biggest problem, and more drugs were just going to make things worse. She could see the boy that she'd raised had returned since the sharp shock of institutionalisation, so what was the point in stretching out this pointless 'treatment' for some disease that was only in his head? He'd never be normal so long as he needed medication to make him normal, so if she could just wean him off it, then he would be fine.

His dosages were reduced between the pharmacy counter and the pillbox at home. When he attended his doctor's appointments, he began expressing concerns over a constant headache, likely a side effect of withdrawal but that he was increasingly convinced was a symptom of a blood clot in his brain. Given the unknown nature of his pain and the potential side effects of his medication, a computerised brain scan was undertaken, discovering that there was nothing neurologically wrong with Rick's brain.

In 1977, the time came for Rick's conservatorship to be renewed in court, but feeling that her son had now made a full recovery and could attend to his own concerns, Beatrice allowed it to lapse.

Almost immediately after he regained legal control over his life, Rick cancelled the payment of his rent and terminated his lease. More than a thousand dollars in back payments of his Social Security had accrued in his account, and he intended to take a trip up to Washington to celebrate the return of his freedom. His mother was supportive of the idea, giving him several hundred dollars from her savings and encouraging him to get away and clear his head of all the bad things that had happened in his past.

In June, he took a Greyhound bus up north and did not return for three weeks. He spent the first couple of weeks in Washington taking in what passed for the sights and listening to the ever-louder cacophony of conflicting voices in his head. By the third week, his old wanderlust had returned, and he headed down to Colorado in search of some fresh ideas and inspiration.

In Steamboat Springs, luck brought him in contact with a man looking to sell his car, and for the low price of all the money that he had left on him, he came away with his very own silver Ford Ranchero pick-up truck. A car of his very own. He drove the car back home to his mother's house feeling both safer and more untethered than he had in years. He could break and run whenever he wanted to. Whenever things got to be too much for him, he could hop in his car and go. He had an escape route from his whole life planned out, so there was no more need to hide the truth.

Wild Dog

In his absence, Beatrice had made some changes around the house. The biggest of these changes was a German Shepherd puppy. The family had never had pets before, for obvious reasons, but now that Rick was out there in the world and Beatrice was all alone, she felt a lack of companionship and protection. The plan was for her to raise the puppy to adulthood and so get herself a fearsome-looking guard dog and a friend. Rick didn't like it. Animals had a strange reaction to him when he wasn't actively trying to lure them. It kept positioning itself between him and his mother, hackles rising when he raised his voice. There would be no hitting or intimidating her as long as that dog was around.

A stray cat had also made her garden its home during this time, and Beatrice delighted in the way that it played with the puppy to the degree that she'd begun leaving food out for the animal. It was like Rick was being haunted by the ghosts of all the animals he'd killed in his youth.

He stayed with his mother for only a couple of weeks after his trip. He could not tolerate the new home that his mother had made, with all of its reminders of his darkest fantasies. Fantasies that had been coming back more and more since he'd been weaned entirely off his medication. He knew in his gut that he needed to replenish his supply of life force. He could feel himself fading more and more every day as all his old aches and pains returned.

The Nazis had infiltrated his school when he was younger, explaining his poor grades and the various ways that he had been poisoned through the years. They were bombarding him even now with their psychic messages, telling him to give up and die, telling him to lash out and kill the people that were on his side so that they could isolate him further. They had to get rid of him because he knew about their UFOs, he knew about Operation Paperclip bringing all the Nazi scientists over to work in Area 51, where they'd developed the technology to fly without propulsion and shrink people's hearts with their death rays and poisoned soap dishes. They had agents everywhere, and all that he had to fight back with was his psychic power, diluted by the medication that Nazi doctors had been forcing on him when they were meant to be curing the food poisoning from that bad rabbit. He had to stay healthy or he'd fall into their hands again. He needed to replenish his life force. He needed blood. He needed to kill.

Beatrice returned home to an eerie silence. The usual joyful barking of the puppy was nowhere to be heard, nor was Rick's now-familiar bitching and moaning about how loud it was. The dog was not bouncing by the front door, nor could she hear it in the back garden. A cold weight settled in Beatrice's guts as she walked by the bathroom and saw Rick painstakingly washing his hands, scrubbing every nail with a brush, soap lathered up to his elbows. There were still flecks of rust in his eyebrows and eyelashes. Missed when he'd washed his face.

She rushed out to the back garden to find her precious puppy in ruins. Rick had not killed the dog. He didn't have the courage to go against his mother's wishes so directly as that, but he had mutilated it beyond recognition, while still leaving it alive. It would not be staring at him and judging with those big brown eyes anymore. It would not be perking up its ears to track his coming and going. It would not be sniffing out his deceptions or wagging its tail when it was rewarded for keeping him at bay. It would not be biting anyone, even playfully. He had taken everything that he did not like away from the dog. The veterinarians did what they could for the animal, but ultimately it had to be put down.

Rick did not wait to be asked to leave. He had already made arrangements to return to the Watt Avenue Complex, to a different apartment. Yet still, he didn't feel like his work at his mother's house was done. After a few weeks with no contact between them, Beatrice was startled to hear someone knocking on her door. Rick was there, with the stray cat's dead body in his hands. He was letting out a long drawn-out moan in anticipation of his mother's own sobs and screams, but when she just stood there in stony silence, he felt compelled to push further. He pressed his fingers into the cold body of the dead cat and ripped it in half, prying open its ribcage in a shower of blood and organs, then smearing the blood from his hands onto his face while maintaining eye contact with Beatrice throughout it all.

Even as he let the tattered remains of her cat fall to the ground in broad daylight, Beatrice could not bring herself to show weakness. She'd lived for years with a bullying man forcing out her sobs – she wasn't going to give Rick the satisfaction of knowing that he'd upset her. After he left unsatisfied, she buried the cat in the garden and never spoke a word about it to anyone. Like so many of the warning signs about Rick's mental deterioration, it could have caused Beatrice embarrassment, so it was summarily ignored.

Now that he was alone and himself again, Rick began to conduct further research into the Nazi conspiracy that was targeting him. He became convinced that he had found evidence of somebody else who was working against them and tried to contrive some way to contact the Hillside Strangler.

The Strangler, actually two men working in concert unbeknownst to the media reporting on it at the time, was a serial killer in Los Angeles who had been strangling young women to death. While the reasons for the Stranglers' crimes were entirely unrelated to Rick's obsession with life-force and blood, it tied into his delusion that he was a victim of a widespread and powerful conspiracy.

With the mutilation of his mother's dog, he had returned to the hunting habits of his youth. Rabbits had served their purpose, but he could still remember the fresh thrills of killing larger animals like cats and dogs. He would never recapture that feeling he had as a teenager, discovering his body, his vices, and their fulfilment. Too much time had passed, and he had delved too deeply into darker habits for the old killings to arouse him the same way. Still, they served well enough for meat and blood. He preyed on the neighbourhood dogs for as long as it escaped notice, only stopping when the police began asking questions, trying to ascertain if there was some sort of wild animal roaming the streets of Sacramento by night. Everywhere that Rick went, there seemed to be signs posted for missing dogs. As a child, he'd been oblivious to them, but now the eyes of every cat and dog he'd killed were staring out at him in black and white on every street corner and every lamppost. He tore some down, but that too started to attract attention. He needed to make the posters go away. He couldn't bear the dead animal eyes on him, the judgement, the knowledge that all those people were hunting for him, trying to track him down. He had to make it stop. He had to make them stop.

The simplest solution was to call the numbers. All the numbers on all the fliers posted all over town, everywhere that he had roamed and hunted and drawn the lifeblood that sustained him even now.

One by one, the owners of missing cats and dogs received phone calls, some during the day, some in the dead of night, because Rick had no real sense of the passage of time. If the owners of the dead animals were unfortunate enough to answer, then what would follow was less of an apology and more of a session of gloating. Rick would tell them to stop looking for their pet, that it was dead, and if they showed any hint of doubt, then he would proceed to detail every part of the poor animal's death in gruesome detail. Many of the people receiving these calls went on to report them to the police, but the police had no reason to believe that the perpetrator of the calls actually had anything to do with the missing animals. The fliers stopped being posted and Rick slipped under the radar.

He began to hoard weaponry once again, various hunting rifles that he justified as necessary for his need for fresh meat along with pistols for self-defence against the shadowy groups that were out to get him. He piled up most of this arsenal in his car for 'hunting trips' and soon began heading out on long drives while he contemplated how he could secure his health. It was during one of these multi-day outings that he found himself in Nevada, driving along motorways for hours through the stretches of desert, trying to surround himself with nothingness so that some of it might enter his troubled mind through osmosis. His downward spiral had been accelerating with time. His father had always provided some sense of stability to his life, even as his mother encouraged him to spin further out of control, but now he had lost all trust in the man. He'd been betrayed one time too many, and he didn't trust Richard Senior not to turn him in to another mental hospital if their paths crossed.

That degeneration of his mental state was accompanied by a new wash of 'symptoms' that he found himself suffering from – pains and aches he couldn't explain. Headaches, tremors, palpitations. All the symptoms that someone suffering from an anxiety disorder is likely to encounter.

His attempts to contact the Hillside Strangler to beg for help in his own struggle had been childish, ill-conceived, and abandoned almost as soon as he'd formulated them. He was on his own against the Nazi conspiracy. He had to do whatever was necessary to hold them off even as they shrunk his heart and evaporated his blood to dust.

Out in Nevada, there were no pets for him to hunt, no way for him to replenish his life force. He could feel his terror and weakness building up inside him. He needed blood, fresh blood to replace all that the Nazis were burning away. He needed to kill or he was going to be killed. Surely there was no evil in that, no wickedness in survival.

In the dwindling hours of the day, not far from the Pyramid Lake Reservation, he came upon a cattle farm - the perfect opportunity to revive himself. Killing a cow was not like killing smaller animals. His bare hands were not sufficient. He had to use a rifle, a knife, and all of his rebuilt strength to drain blood from the dead heifer's carcass and dig out its liver.

He filled up a plastic bucket with its blood, but he was very aware of how exposed he was here on the side of the road. The Nazis' allies or the farmer might come rolling along at any moment, drawn here by the gunshot, cattle cries, or his own ecstatic moaning. Darkness was descending now, and under its cover, he'd be able to renew himself in peace.

He let the road guide him, as he often did, following along the twists and turns until he came to the side of Pyramid Lake a little after midnight. The moon shone high above him, like the eye of the Nazis up there, staring right down at him. He needed to be protected from that gaze. He needed to get as much of the cow's life force into his body as he could. He drank blood from the bucket until his stomach was fit to burst, and when even that wasn't enough, he started smearing the gore all over his skin. It wasn't enough. Nothing was enough. He stripped out of his clothes and covered every inch of his body in blood, using the stolen liver like a sponge. Hadn't he read somewhere that the liver was like a sponge? Wouldn't this be enough to purify him? To wash away the evil that they'd put inside him. Would this hide him from their eyes? From the sensors of their UFOs? He had to know. He was still weak and his blood was still evaporating so fast he could feel it drying tacky on his skin, but he had to know if they were still watching. He roamed out onto the beach, heading along to an outcropping of rocks where there was no way that he could be mistaken for anything else. He threw out his arms and he screamed up at the flying saucers circling overhead – screaming his defiance and his hate. He was going to survive. Whatever it took, he was going to live.

The police found him like that not long afterwards, discovering the arsenal of weapons and the bloody bucket in his car along with all his clothing and worldly possessions. He was taken into custody, and there was every expectation that he would be up on murder charges even if it was apparent that he would be found not guilty by cause of insanity. It was only after forensics reported that his 'victim' had been nothing more than a cow, and that he'd likely sourced the blood and organs from a butcher, that all charges were dropped and he was released into his recognisance.

Once more, he slipped under the radar and out of sight, considered too ridiculous and outlandish to actually pose any real threat to anyone.

On his return home, with several of his illegally acquired weapons still impounded by the police until he could provide them with proper documentation to prove his ownership, Rick was feeling bereft. The cow had given up its life to him, to protect him from harm, and then the police working with the Nazi conspiracy had gassed all that goodness right out of him again while he was sleeping in his cell. His heart was so shrunken now that if any of those Nazi collaborating doctors ever took the time to scan him, they'd have a hard time even seeing it. He needed to do more. He needed to fight back somehow. But first he had to arm himself.

On December 2, 1977, Rick purchased a new semi-automatic .22 pistol for cash but could not take it home until his credentials could be verified. He politely accepted these terms but was internally seething that even in America, the land of the free, he had to jump through hoops for his right to bear arms. It had to be the Nazi influence. He'd read that they'd tried to disarm the populace before their ascent to power in other places too. This had to be a sign that they were about to put their takeover into action. He had to get his strength back or he wouldn't be able to fight them. Nobody else even believed that the Nazis were trying to take over America – he had to stand alone against them until the whole world saw his bravery and joined up with him. All this time they'd been looking down on him, hating him and doubting him, but someday they'd look up from their squalor and see him shining there like the hero he was: the man who'd done what needed to be done to keep the world safe.

He picked up his new gun and stowed it away safely in the glove compartment of his car. It was almost time for his war to begin, but he still needed to practice before he could launch his counterattack.

At first, he had been weakened by the lack of dogs available for him to hunt and kill around the neighbourhood. Even the strays that sometimes came through seemed to be avoiding his patch of town, but luckily he was not the only one hunting those animals down. The SPCA had been picking up strays during his absence in Nevada, explaining his poor pickings, but luckily they were more than happy to part with the animals 'to a good home' in exchange for a small donation. For $15 Rick got himself a pair of decent-sized dogs and brought them home. Their blood, and a slurry of their food-processed organs, returned some of Rick's strength to him, but after the cow, they seemed like a pale imitation of the real thing. He needed to kill something with more life energy if he was going to be ready to fight the Nazi UFOs. He needed to kill a human being.

It didn't frighten him. Maybe it would have before bodies became machinery to be taken apart when the time called for it, but now, after fighting his enemies and his own body all these years, it just seemed to be necessary.

He drove around town in his car, not planning anything, just watching for the right opportunity. Hoping that it would come soon. Supremely aware of the ticking time bomb of his precarious health. His heart shrunk ever smaller as he waited and waited.

On December 27, he finally saw his opportunity. He caught a glimpse of a pretty woman through the bay window of one of the suburban homes he'd rolled by who reminded him of how his mother had looked when she was younger. Back when she was still pretty and his father hadn't beaten all the joy out of her. He pulled out one of his .22 pistols and fired.

The shot missed, shattering a pane of glass and lodging in the wooden door frame by his potential victim's feet. Rick did not attempt a second shot. He put his foot down, tearing away before anybody could try to intervene. He cursed himself all the way. Stupid. Stupid and twitchy. He'd had the chance there to really do something. To really make a difference. His whole body had risen up in anticipation of the blood, his confusing libido flaring to life alongside all of the aches and pains that told him that, for the moment at least, he was still alive. He slunk off into the shadows with his whole mind inflamed with all the feelings he'd spent a lifetime hiding from, leaving all the little people to pick through the consequences of what he'd done.

A rapid police response found the slug embedded in the kitchen door frame, but there was no other evidence or explanation for the inexplicable shooting. With nobody hurt and no real case to pursue, the evidence was passed off to the ballistics forensic team to be filed and then forgotten. The shooting did not even make the news.

Rick was going berserk. He had been so close to starting his glorious crusade against the space Nazi conspiracy that he could taste it, yet here he was with no blood on his hands except the remains of the last dog that he still hadn't quite finished processing. It was a stopgap measure, and he knew it. When he'd been aiming down that barrel, a rush of life energy had filled him up. He'd known what it was like to be alive again. He couldn't melt back into death without even trying. He had to try again.

Even the usual routines that Rick had once used to calm himself were stripped away from him. His sister was returning to the family home for Christmas dinner, but her condition for coming was that Rick would not attend. Facing this ultimate rejection from his mother was enough to light a fresh flare of rage inside of him.

He started driving around Sacramento all over again, street by street, house by house, just waiting for the perfect victim to present himself. Everywhere he went, his shots were obscured. Too far away to hit. Too close to witnesses. Too plain and uninteresting. The victim had to be right. He couldn't just gun down some kid playing hopscotch. He had to feel like he was being invited to do it. Like his sense of justice was commanding him.

Ambrose Griffin was a 51-year-old engineer. A married man with two children. He was red in the face when Rick saw him, arms full of the groceries that he was carrying into the house for his wife. He did not look like Rick's father. There was no physical resemblance whatsoever. Yet somehow, his mind connected the two. Here was his ultimate betrayer, out in the open, just begging for justice to be done. There was nobody else in the street. Nobody else in the world. Just Rick in his car and Ambrose turning from the back seat to face the street head-on, his chest perfectly framed by brown paper bags. Everything was aligned. Rick took aim and squeezed the trigger without hesitation. Ambrose fell like a puppet that had its strings cut.

That was how Rick justified it to himself later, in his more lucid moments. This man was just a puppet of the conspiracy, and he had set him free.

Rick's pick-up truck screeched off down the road and around the corner just as people rushed out to see what the bang had been. Like a ghost, he was gone before his victim had even died.

This time, when the police flooded the neighbourhood around Robertson Avenue, they could not simply brush the crime under the rug, nor did they have any intention of doing so. They canvassed everyone in the area and gave Ambrose's body the full forensic treatment. Ambrose's son was the only one to provide anything resembling a lead. Earlier in the day, he had seen a neighbour wandering the streets with a .22-calibre rifle. The police swarmed the poor squirrel hunter, confiscating his rifle and throwing him into a cell until the ballistics could be analysed.

The rifle did not match the shot that had killed Ambrose. No .22-calibre weapon registered in the state of California matched that ballistic profile. If the work had been done faster, then the .22 slug plucked out of the door frame just a few streets away would have been matched to the same weapon. If Rick's school friends had not concealed the pistol that he'd brought to their party, then there would have been a matching record that would have immediately led to his arrest for this murder. Once again, the whole universe seemed to bend to mask Rick's hand in his crimes and help him to avoid detection. It is easy to understand why he felt like his path was destiny when everything contrived to protect him.

A Hero's Welcome

Rick was alive for the first time in his memory. His body was awash with blood, and he was breathing deeply without a hitch in his chest. He was alive and feeling all the things that a man felt.

On January 11, he bumped into one of his neighbours, Dawn Larson, in the complex as she was heading home from her night shift. As politely as he could manage, he demanded that Dawn give him one of her cigarettes, yet even when she complied, he crowded her into a corner on the stairwell, thanking her for her kindness with a monotone voice that spoke more of threats than gratitude. Eventually, she handed him the whole pack of cigarettes, but his roving eyes and looming presence did not stop. He was reaching out towards her chest when the clomping feet of another of their neighbours distracted him and he broke away, leaving her to flee back to her apartment, just across the hall from his, in terror.

He bought a copy of the Sacramento Bee with the details of his shooting and the societal condemnation of the random violence spread across the front page. While all the other papers and books in his home were in a constant state of disarray, this one page he kept pristine and perfect – although the print began to rub away at the edges from where he constantly handled it, staring down at the black-and-white evidence that what he had done was real, that everything that he had ever thought or believed was not the product of his imagination, but of a reality that the weak of mind were too afraid to face.

Now that he was full of vital energy once more, Rick felt like his car was an unnecessary addition to his roaming routine. On a practical level, he felt like it would make him easier to identify and connect with his previous killing, and on an emotional level, he felt like it held him too far separate from the rhythms of the world. It also forced him into a physical distance from his targets that interfered with his enjoyment of the kill. He wanted to combine the best parts of killing animals with the overwhelming rush that he got from killing people. He wanted to feel the meat of their bodies, still hot in his hands. He wanted to look into their eyes as the life left their bodies. All of the things he had never been able to do with girls, he could do then. All the joys that life was meant to bring but that had been denied to him by the poisons and illnesses of his past could finally be his.

He roamed the streets on foot, passing through invisibly, just another young hippy-looking guy going about his business in peace. If someone had been following after him then, they would have seen that every so often, he would walk up to the door of a house and try it to see if it was unlocked. Most of the doors were. For the people in the neighbourhoods that he was trawling through, he probably just looked like a visitor, or one of the seemingly endless pseudo-protestors roaming around with their clipboards looking for signatures on this campaign or that petition. Whales needed saving. Trees needed to be protected. Rick needed no excuse to be where he was.

It was almost two weeks after the killing of Ambrose Griffin that Rick's bizarre behaviour was noticed. A woman staying alone in her home throughout the day heard somebody try to open her front door, then watched as Rick walked right past all of her windows in plain view. She heard him try the back door, then crept over to the window to watch him wander off across her garden and hop a fence into her neighbour's property. She called the police, but this far from the site of the last murder, and with so different an MO, the police paid it little attention, suggesting that she call if he came around again.

On and on Rick walked. Never slowing except to try a door here or there. His invisibility was not perfect, however. He froze at the sound of his name being called out.

Nancy Holden had attended school with Rick, never falling into the trap of a relationship with him, but close enough to many of his other girlfriends to be on first-name terms. She had pulled up at the side of the road at the odd sight of him wandering around aimlessly, and finally called him over when it didn't seem like he was going to notice her on his own. The two of them chatted briefly, with Rick sidestepping too many questions about how he'd been spending his adult life, and Nancy making her own assumptions based on the look of him and the fact that she could smell him at six feet away.

The coolness that had always drawn people to Rick seemed to have melted away with the years, and now all of his hungers were laid bare for anyone to see if they took the time to speak to him. His eyes roved over Nancy as they spoke, never meeting her eyes but locking on to many other parts of her for extended awkward silences. Eventually, he began angling for her to give him a lift home.

Despite the social contract that she subscribed to, some old instinct was screaming in the back of Nancy's head. She would not offer Rick a ride. She didn't want his skin-crawling gaze or his skin-crawling stench in her private space. Not any more than she would have invited a rat or cockroach to share a ride with her. When he was denied, Rick became angry, still trying to cajole Nancy to obey him without raising his voice but doing a poor job of both tasks. Eventually, she drove away, leaving him standing fuming at the side of the road, and leaving a lasting impression in her mind that something was seriously wrong with that man.

A few streets away, Rick found what he was looking for. An unlocked door was an invitation for him to come in. They wanted him to go in. They wanted him to do his work in this house. If they didn't, they would have locked the door.

Inside he was expecting the residents to be lined up and waiting for him to dole out their punishment for serving the Nazis, but there was nobody to be seen. The house had been left unlocked and empty. Rick crept forwards, peering into room after room. Letting memories echo down inside the black void where his mind used to be.

There were baby toys and baby clothes everywhere. Some child, some bastard child, had been brought into this world, and here it was being pampered. The spoiled little brat would never have to cower and hide from the fists of its father or sip poison from its mother's teat. It would live a long safe life, protected from the Nazi UFOs by the parents' complicity, never knowing that the whole world that it lived in was built on lies and shit.

Well, he could break some part of the illusion for the boy, even if the parents never did. Rick hauled down his trousers and squatted over the baby's cot, squeezing excrement out, then wiping his ass clean with a patchwork blanket. Next, he hauled open one of the drawers and pissed all over the kid's clothes. This would teach the boy a lesson. Teach him not to talk back to Daddy. Not to listen to his mother. Not to believe all the lies that they told him. If somebody had come in and warned Rick about all this, then he might have been saved. He might have escaped before they could poison him or the police Nazis could gas him and shrink his heart.

The kid would get in trouble for shitting and pissing all over its room. The parents would look down on him with total disgust and hatred, just like he'd seen in his parents' eyes every time he wet the bed. He hoped they beat the kid stupid for making all this mess. He hoped it cried and cried and its bones broke and they tore it apart like a rabbit. They would be deceived, and the boy would be broken into his component pieces, and somewhere out in the city, unseen, Rick would feel the flood of life energy filling up his body. He was already hard just imagining that rush.

That was when the family came home.

It was immediately apparent that their home had been broken into – Rick left a trail of chaos in his wake everywhere that he went, knocking things down, rifling through drawers, always searching for some evidence to back up his paranoid delusions. While the wife and child hung back in the doorway, the father, bold protector, went charging in, catching Rick in the face with his first punch and never slowing. Rick had to dive to the floor and scurry like an animal to avoid the avenging father's fury – subhuman once more as some father figure rained down fury, justice, and pain. Rick pushed his way past, bounded on all fours through the hallway, and made it back to his feet just in time to unlock the back door and flee for his life.

This time, the police had no idea what to make of the bizarre report. It was clearly unrelated to the murder just a few streets away, so the priority was low, but once again, the family were encouraged to call if they saw anything else unusual. No forensic evidence was taken from the scene beyond a few photographs, mostly to assure the couple's insurance company that the event had actually taken place.

Rick had already been flooded with energy and strength that he hadn't felt in years, but now his old companion rage made its way back to the surface. He had never been alive and enraged before, it was a strange combination of experiences. He found that his skin was almost crackling with the barely contained energy. Still, he knew that soon it would have an outlet. Each door that he tried brought him closer to the right one. The one that would give him his revelation and ascension. The one that would heal him and make him whole again.

In the meantime, he continued to keep up his strength by slaughtering animals. Watching through her peephole, Dawn Larson saw him bringing three dogs into the apartment in one afternoon – even though none ever seemed to come out again. Ever since their encounter in the stairwell, she had been careful to watch his comings and goings to make sure that their paths would not cross, but the patterns of behaviour that were emerging were truly bizarre.

Two of the dogs that she had watched Rick bringing home that day were puppies that he had purchased from a family nearby. The other was a puppy that he had stolen from someone's yard on his way home with his new acquisitions. The next morning, the family that had sold him the puppies woke up to a horrifying sight. Both of the dogs had been returned to them, dumped at the edge of their lawn, dead and completely drained of all their blood. The stolen four-month-old puppy was not returned. Rick shot it in the head for barking at him, then blended its internal organs down into a slurry that he drank raw every time he felt himself weakening.

On January 23, he found another unlocked door. The Wallin family lived at 2630 Tioga Way. They were another young couple, like so many of Richard's chosen victims – currently childless, although Theresa Wallin was three months pregnant and getting ready to tell friends and family the good news. She and Rick passed each other in the street as she was taking out a bag of trash. As always, he was invisible to the normal people of Sacramento. He strolled right by her, up her driveway, and walked straight into her house without hesitation. She didn't even see him. Nobody ever saw him.

After dumping the black plastic bag in the bin by the curb, she turned back home without a care in the world, ambling up the path with her hand on her stomach. There was no bump yet, not with her first pregnancy at the age of twenty-two, but she imagined that she could feel the baby moving inside her. That she could feel it growing and coming alive.

She was so distracted that she'd walked into the house and shut the door before she realised that anything was awry. Rick was standing in her hallway with his pistol levelled at her head. She opened her mouth to speak, but no words came. She tried to lift her hands, as though they could stop what was coming, as if she could turn aside bullets. The first shot hit her in the left hand, the second in the forehead. She was dead before she hit the ground. Rick calmly placed the gun against her temple and pulled the trigger one last time, just to be sure. This was his first time killing a woman. His first time being close enough to one that he could feel the heat radiating off her body. An orgasm rocked him, robbing him of his strength and his senses. He stayed there, hunched over her corpse, shuddering and moaning as the whole world faded to white noise. The rush was unlike anything he'd ever experienced. The best experience in his whole life, taking life from someone else.

From there, Rick's actions became methodical rather than impassioned. His lusts fulfilled and a steady flow of life energy now trickling through the air from the bullet holes and into his body, he now just had to complete his duty to ensure that his efforts had all been worthwhile. He needed to feed to fight off the sickness.

Taking a hold on Teresa, he hauled her body through to the bedroom, straining to hoist her up onto the bed, then fastidiously removed all of her clothes and laid them to one side. It was the first time he had seen a woman without clothes on. All of his previous teenage fumblings had involved only a partial state of undress as they were hurried and secretive. Now he had the time to take in all the sights. Yet his lusts were not stirred. His rage against this woman and all the others like her still boiled just beneath the surface of his skin, but it was accompanied not by a desire to possess or use this body but to destroy and desecrate it. He found the kitchen and retrieved an empty yoghurt carton and a butcher's knife along with the mop bucket from under the sink.

With the knife, he began at the area of his most interest. Slicing her left nipple clean off her body and setting it aside, then squeezing her breast to milk what blood he could out of her into the yoghurt carton. This woman was his mother, giving him life to drink from her bosom. He milked at the dead breast until no more blood was flowing, then he guzzled the carton's worth down.

Life filled him. Salty and sweet and real. His heart swelled and beat once more. He could feel every inch of stickiness and sweat all over his body. This too had to be cleansed. This too had to be set right.

He made an incision just below the breastbone and sliced the skin, fat, and muscle away from Teresa's torso cavity in a single cut, all the way down to her left hip. He had angled the cut for a reason. The bucket was positioned at the left side of the bed to collect the blood as it flowed down that angled cut. He let her drain for a time, molesting her corpse while he waited. Dipping his fingers in and out of her as gently as he could. Moving from one hole to the next, trying to rekindle the spark of rage and lust that he had experienced in the hall. It did not work, he was spent.

When the blood seemed to slow, he returned to his work, carefully pulling aside the intestines so that he could get to the organs that they hid. He severed both kidneys and took them out of her body for examination, snipped a section of the small intestine away and ate it raw as he thought through his next step.

This was his first time with a full human body to examine, and no matter how many books he'd read on the subject, nothing quite prepared him for the complexity of it. He dug around inside Teresa's corpse with both hands, the way he used to tear up cats and birds when he was younger. When he came upon her uterus and realised that it looked different to the ones he'd seen in the photographs of his medical textbooks, he excised it. With the tip of the knife, he opened it up and looked at what he suspected was hidden inside. The foetus was as dead as its mother. Lifeless and still in the palm of his hand.

It would never know fear. It would never sicken. He had saved it from all of that. He was a hero. He'd done for this child what nobody had ever done for him, protecting it from a lifetime of torment and dread. To be sure, he cut the foetus into three equally sized parts, then returned it to first the uterus, then to the body.

He returned both kidneys to the body too, placing them just below her liver, which he also opted to leave in place after putting in all the work of opening her up and digging around for it. He was feeling better than he had in his entire life. He didn't need any more for now. His insides were all working just fine – only his outsides needed work.

Taking the bucket of blood to the bathroom, Rick poured it all over himself, massaging it into his skin and luxuriating as he felt all the grime and weakness washing away. He was himself again. He was alive.

He showered off the sticky residue of Teresa's life in her en suite shower, then he took her nipple as a little memento of a very pleasant day. He popped it into his mouth and began to chew on it as he walked out of her house and into the garden. Her dog remained chained up at the far end of the plot of land, cowering in its dog house from the worst of the afternoon sun. Rick wasn't here for it. He had no more use for dogs. They were beneath him. Loathsome creatures, just like Teresa had been. He crouched down in the grass beside a dried heap of dog excrement, and he smiled. This was a fitting end for all the mothers who thought they could control their sons. A fitting end for all the women who'd laughed behind his back because he couldn't get it up. He could get it up now. Oh, they would all see that soon enough.

With a handful of dog shit, he returned to the bedroom to take in the sight of what he had achieved. Teresa lay spread-eagle across the bed like a whore waiting for her next customer. Guts and mouth hanging wide open. He pushed the dog shit past her teeth and down into her throat before wiping what was left of it on her pillow. This was what they all deserved. All the women. Everyone who worked for the Nazis to control him and tame him and poison him. So, unto all tyrants.

When he emerged onto the street, he was invisible once more. He was full of life, yet he felt oddly drained. Rage had always sustained him, but today, he was bereft of it. There was an echoing void inside him where his hate and anger usually dwelled. It was like he had died a little death along with his victim.

It was only then that he came to the inevitable conclusion that his rage was a part of his sickness. When he felt hatred and anger, it wasn't because he was bad. It wasn't because he wanted to kill and hurt people. It was the Nazi poison, making him do terrible things to survive. It all made sense now, and

Rick was absolved of all guilt. They were making him do this to survive them, but they were also making him want to do this. It was perfect.

When Teresa's husband returned home, it was to a scene out of a nightmare. The police were only summoned after neighbours heard his screams of anguish and rushed to help. The pain that Rick caused to the living is never really considered. His mutilations were committed against dead bodies that could not fight back, but the pain he caused stretched far beyond the bodies that he rent.

Ballistics matched the gun used in this killing to the murder of Ambrose Griffin, and Rick had left fingerprints in blood all over the scene, meaning that if and when the police did finally capture him, there would be no difficulty in linking him to the murder. Sadly, despite his time incarcerated across multiple states through the years, and all of his time in mental hospitals, Rick's fingerprints had never been added to any sort of centralised database.

Blood Orgy

In the aftermath of this first fully realised murder, Rick was filled with confidence that he would be able to commit others just as smoothly and invisibly. He spent his days fantasising about what he would do next time, now that he knew just what was involved and how his body would react. He found that his intermingled lust and rage would return during these bouts of fantasy.

It took only three days before his hunger returned in full and he started stalking the streets again. On January 27, 1978, he found another unlocked door, welcoming him in.

The house on 3207 Merrywood Drive was bursting with life when Rick walked in. Dan Meredith had popped in for a visit from next door, and he was watching over the kids while Evelyn Miroth took a quick bath. Evelyn's six-year-old son Jason was as excited as ever for a visit from 'Uncle Dan', while her 22-month-old nephew David was mesmerised by the strange man who was rolling a ball back and forth across the living room floor. As he was in his fifties, Dan's children were grown up now but still a little young for bringing home grandkids for him to babysit, so Dan enjoyed opportunities like this to help out Evelyn.

At the sound of the front door opening, Dan was surprised but not worried. Evelyn's sister might have been coming around early to pick up her kid. Evelyn's husband might have been coming back. But when nobody called out, he pulled himself to his feet and left the children alone to go and check who had just let themselves in.

Rick already had his gun up and trained on Dan when he came into the entryway. At point-blank range, he pulled the trigger, splattering the man's brains across the pastel walls. As the body fell, the screaming started. Rick paused at the body only long enough to tug a wallet from the dead man's back pocket and check he was dead before moving forward. In the living room, he caught a glimpse of Jason as he ran out of the room. Rick pursued him, casually shooting the baby in the face as he passed.

In Evelyn's bedroom, Jason was cornered. Rick pressed the gun to the back of the cowering boy's head and pulled the trigger twice. More blood and brains splattered the walls. Rick did not slow. These deaths did not matter. They were just steps on the path to his true objective. They meant nothing.

Putting his shoulder to the door, Rick burst into the bathroom where Evelyn still lay in the water. It was every fantasy fulfilled. His willing victim already laid out nude for him, just waiting for his delicate ministrations. Evelyn was 38 years old, still beautiful, and at just the age of Rick's mother when he began to turn against her. Even her dark hair in the water reminded him of Beatrice and the brief glimpses of pale flesh through the cracked bathroom door.

He fired into her forehead, punching a perfect hole through the middle of her skull, keeping her perfect apart from that one little mark and its partner, hidden by her hair.

Rick stopped then, listening for the sounds of any other living thing in the house, sniffing at the air. There was nothing. His lust still burned, not depleted in the least by these mechanical murders. All his time lost in fantasy had paid off, and now he could do what he had always wanted.

Evelyn's corpse was dragged through to her bedroom, and Rick tossed her face down onto the bed. From this angle, she looked like she was still alive and undamaged. Still perfect but for the scent of blood. In the kitchen, he found a knife, then he went to work.

On the back of Evelyn's neck, he made a small incision that welled up with blood at once. He latched onto it, drinking and sucking the hot life force right out of her. His lips tingled. His whole body stiffened. He was alive. This was what he needed. This was what he had always needed.

His own cadaverous body was draped over her like they were lovers in an embrace, and as Rick sucked at her neck, he rocked back and forth against her, the cooling flesh and his clothes providing him with the friction that he needed to maintain his erection throughout the whole process. When the wound on her neck stopped producing blood, he turned her head to face the opposite way and made another matching cut on the opposite side. Blood trickled down her back, and he dragged his tongue up the length of her spine to capture it. Just like that, he seemed to realise that his greatest fantasies could now be fulfilled. He had a woman here, naked and ready for him. He had the blood and the life that it gave him.

He struggled his trousers down to his knees, then pushed himself inside Evelyn's unresisting body. He drooped back over her to latch onto the welling blood at her neck. With every suck of the blood, his hips jerked spasmodically forward. He had failed to find his target in his rape of the corpse, pushing into Evelyn's anus instead of his initial goal, but the heat and friction were more than sufficient to keep him moving and panting.

Inside his mind, Rick was close to achieving his ascension. Everything had led him to this moment. All the misery and pain and death. All the years he was ground down to dirt by the world, abused by the people who were meant to love him, targeted by the Nazi conspiracy for death. It had all led him here to this one moment when all that he had ever been and all that he could ever be crossed paths. He was perfected.

Orgasms rocked his body, over and over. Each time the flow of blood slowed, he would rear up and make a fresh cut before latching on and fucking away all over again. Time lost all meaning. All that he knew was the cyclical flow of blood in through his mouth and pure bliss out through his cock. He lost track of how many times his whole world faded to white and he had to catch his breath before opening a new wound and resuming his sodomy. Rick probably would have stayed there forever, lurching back and forth between one moment of bliss and the next, if the cold hadn't started to seep in.

By the time he decoupled himself from Evelyn, she was cold, and he could feel the chill of death spreading up his bloodied body, too. He tugged his clothes back on as he realised that this too was another trap, another poison that women used to weaken him. All this time he'd been so desperate to suckle at this poisoned pleasure, and now he was feeling the results. He was exhausted and drained. All the good that the fresh blood had done him had been drained away.

He thrust the knife into the hole that had been giving him so much pleasure until only a moment ago, furiously ripping the blade out and ramming it back into the dead woman's corpse. He flipped her over, staring into her dead face and snarling as he stabbed her all about her torso until every inch of her was marked. It was only then that Rick's version of sanity began to reassert itself. He could fix this.

A long incision from breastbone to pubis opened Evelyn up, and a mixing bowl from the kitchen served to collect all the blood that had been pooling in her torso. He brought it up to his lips reverentially when the work was done, sipping then gulping down the cold blood in great mouthfuls. He would not bathe in her blood – he would make it all his own. He would consume her in her entirety, and he would remember the weakness that she had inflicted on him as her life gave him strength.

With a surgeon's precision, he drew her internal organs out one after another, heaping them up in the same bowl that had held her blood until only moments before. Heart, liver, and small intestines were all removed. The lungs were diced up, but he returned them after a moment when he decided that they were too pale-looking to have much life-force contained within them.

A quick search of the kitchen cabinets produced Tupperware containers that he portioned her organs out into, and a cardboard box, which he transferred the remains of the baby David into whole. These were not trophies; they were supplies to be consumed later. The mother and the child both had to be consumed for Rick to feel that the deed was done, but as he returned to Evelyn's bedroom for another round of butchery, he was interrupted by a rap on the unlocked front door.

He scurried through and locked it before anyone could come inside, but they heard him and saw movement inside the house. Any hope he'd had of playing the place off as empty was lost to his panic. More knocking ensued. They knew he was in here. They were coming for him. The Nazi conspiracy had worked out his location, they'd worked out that he was working against them. He had to run. Digging in Dan Meredith's pockets, he found a set of car keys that matched one he could spy parked out in the street. But to get to his escape vehicle, he needed to outwit or outwait whatever agents the conspiracy had sent after him.

Outside of the front door, that doom-laden Nazi agent stood waiting. She was six years old, had her hair in pigtails, and was tired of waiting for her playdate with her neighbour Jason to start. She knocked again and again while Rick and his bag of corpse meats stayed pressed to the floor of the hall, then when she wandered home to complain to her mother, Rick made a break for it, dashing out to Meredith's car, swinging himself and his trophies inside and driving off at full speed, tyres and gearbox screaming all the way.

The little girl brought a neighbour, the neighbour brought the police. There was no question that it was the work of the same man that killed Teresa Wallin and Ambrose Griffin. Even if the massacres had not been identical, then the numerous shoe and handprints left in the blood all over the house would have matched them up.

Nobody could have been prepared for the nightmarish sights to be found within the house. It was enough to push many of the investigating officers to retire shortly afterwards. Yet the nightmare was only beginning for another family. Evelyn's sister, Karen, came looking for her son, having heard nothing of what had happened to her sister. A son who was nowhere to be seen.

A little boy who was now in the hands of this mass murderer. A ticking clock on the investigation that lit a fire under the local police and set them scrambling. A manhunt swept through the town, with every officer going door to door in a desperate search for 'Baby David'. They knocked on Rick's door amid the canvassing, but he did not answer. He had other things to occupy him.

It was now official that Sacramento had a serial killer on their hands, which meant that they finally qualified for assistance from the FBI. Russ Vorpagel and Robert Ressler were deployed from the Behavioural Science Unit to compile a profile to help track the killer down. After studying the crime scenes and finally making the connections between various other crime reports that could be signs of the same killer trying to build his confidence, they presented a profile that was then offered up to the public.

The killer would be a tall man, physically unclean and malnourished, a loner with a history of petty crimes. This description, while not particularly detailed, was linked to the locations of each one of the crimes, both major and minor, that it was believed the killer had committed before being presented to the public in an outreach program unlike any seen in previous cases. Sacramento did not try to hide the monster in its midst to protect its reputation – all that the city cared about was excising this cancer before it could kill again. Because that was the one part of the profile that had not been made public: There was no doubt that the man who had committed the horrific crimes displayed in the Wallin and Miroth homes would kill again, and that his crimes would continue to escalate. Within the anal cavity of Evelyn Miroth, the coroner found an amount of semen that he was forced to describe in his reports as 'remarkable'. There was no way that this killer would be going back to his normal life. This was a serial killer at the beginning of his curve, and he was already committing atrocities on a level it took others years to build up to.

Back in his apartment, Rick was overwhelmed with opportunities. His fridge was well stocked with the organs of the woman he'd killed, and he had the whole body of baby David at his disposal, to do with as he pleased. As it turned out, what pleased him most was to carefully remove the top of the boy's skull and eat his brain matter with a spoon. All of the child's potential was locked away in that brain, all the chances that he'd had for a better life that Rick had snatched away in an instant. Rick wanted that potential back, he wanted to have a healthy mind inside him.

Yet even when all the brain was consumed, Rick still wasn't feeling as alive as he had been latched on to the neck and ass of a dead woman. The sex was what was missing. This kid had never been twisted. He'd never been poisoned. His sex drive wasn't wired for murder and torture. Rick needed it. He needed to take it from the baby. With a pair of kitchen scissors, he severed the toddler's penis. It was his now. Pristine and unbroken. But how could he use it? How could he filter the life-force from the dead body through this unpolluted sex? In the end, he settled for the most literal approach, making incisions where the blood had pooled, and using the severed penis as a straw to suck it out.

As the hunt for Baby David stretched on, day after day, the profile of the killer and kidnapper was spread ever further until finally, five days into the manhunt, it reached the ears of Nancy Holden. Combined with the new information, placing Rick at the site of the breaking, entering, and defecating just a street from where she had last encountered him, she decided it was her duty to report it to the police.

The emergency reporting line that had been set up was drawing in a multitude of similar calls from all across Sacramento. Hippies were not well-liked by the older population, and now there was an opportunity to report them for being unusual looking and having strange habits. The workings of the investigative system ground to a halt with the influx of reports being checked one by one, and it was only Nancy's comparative youth compared to the average caller that made her very mild comments about Rick stand out.

A background check on Richard Chase turned up a registration for a .22-calibre pistol along with many of the other warning signs that the FBI had recommended that the local police look out for – the most substantial lead that the whole manhunt had turned up since the very beginning. Detectives and uniformed officers arrived at Rick's door, hammering on it and demanding that he come out, but there was no reply, even though it was obvious from the noises that there was somebody inside. Rather than risk the life of Baby David, the police withdrew around a corner and waited for Rick to emerge. The hours ticked by with more and more bizarre sounds emerging from the apartment. Ranting, screaming, mechanical sounds.

The police were pinned in place by indecision. If the baby was still alive in that house, Richard could be killing it right now.

If the baby was gone, then he might be destroying the vital evidence that was needed to convict him. If they didn't move soon, all of their efforts could be for nothing.

That was when they heard the lock on Richard's door being turned.

He made it only a few steps into the hall before he was tackled to the floor. The bloodstained cardboard box in his hands was knocked from his grip, and the pistol that he had used to commit his murders tumbled out of it – the unregistered .22 pistol that had slipped under the police radar since he had used it to threaten party-goers in his very first apartment.

A stench swept out over the arresting officers, emanating in equal parts from Richard and the apartment he had just left. The box was not the only thing stained with blood. His hands, his clothes, even his hair was tangled with it.

'That's from dogs. Blood from dogs. I killed some dogs,' he mumbled out as though it was in any way an explanation. Taking Richard into custody was only the first step, however. A quick search of his person turned up no weapons, but Dan Meredith's wallet was tucked in his back pocket, confirming everyone's suspicions that he was their killer.

Even as he was being hauled away downtown, the detectives and the FBI agents who had arrived during the stand-off in the hallway took their first tentative steps into the nightmare world that he had kept hidden behind the apartment complex's nondescript doors.

The walls, floor, and even the ceiling inside his apartment were splattered with dried blood. His refrigerator had so much on it that it seemed to be leaking out of the machine as if it were a living, wounded thing. The blender that Richard used to make his smoothies was on the counter, thick with coagulated blood and still containing the mashed remains of partially decayed human organs. Beside it lay an array of cookware, cutlery, glasses, and dishes, all stained with blood or still containing the residue of it. The kitchen table was covered in anatomical diagrams covered in Richard's pencilled notes, torn from medical textbooks or photocopied in the library. Everything a layman might need to perform an autopsy or to butcher a corpse for its organs.

The fridge contained the worst horrors. Wrapped in tinfoil, the police found slabs of meat harvested from pets in the neighbourhood. In Saran wrap, on a higher shelf, they found the organs that Rick had taken from his victims. Finally, in a Tupperware container, they uncovered what was left of Baby David's brain, robbing them of any hope that the child might still be recovered alive. It would take weeks for forensics teams to make their way through the chaos of Richard's apartment, separating out the conspiracy theory pamphlets from the history books. The medical journals from the UFO sighting reports. All the components of Richard's paranoid delusions were laid out on paper in his apartment, heaped and mangled together into the same chaos that filled his head.

Interviews with Richard proved to be fruitless. He would not speak, or when he did, he spouted out such nonsense that it seemed to be impossible to parse. Psychiatrists were brought in to assess Richard and determine whether he was competent to stand trial. For those men, he was suddenly an open book. All of his nightmares, delusions, and memories of an abusive childhood were brought up and repeated with carefully rehearsed pauses for dramatic effect.

The police watching from the other side of the interrogation room mirror were beside themselves with fury to see the medical professionals dutifully noting everything down and nodding sympathetically. Buying all the murderer's blatant lies – hook, line, and sinker. Yet when the time came for the psychiatrists to file their reports and recommendations, it seemed that the insanity plea that Richard was working up to had failed to take root.

There was too much deception in his storytelling for anything he said to be taken at face value, and he was lucid enough to discuss the morality of his actions while he was simultaneously trying to distance himself from his own part in those actions. There was more than enough evidence to convict Richard without a confession, yet he was willing to make confessions when the police suggested that it might provide a judge with a good reason to be lenient. While he abridged his crimes greatly when confessing, brushing over the sexual drive behind his murders and focusing exclusively on the necessity of his actions to avoid the Nazi-mafia conspiracy that was arrayed against him, he demanded that all of the documentation from his own home, which he had gathered as evidence of that conspiracy, should be presented to his lawyer, and in turn to the court, so that they could see that he was the real victim here. He hoped that on his day in court, the truth about those who had spent their lives tormenting him might be brought to light. At no point did he express any remorse or guilt over the crimes that he had committed. At no point did he even accept responsibility for them, trying to spin tales to justify his actions to whoever would listen, like the floodgates had finally opened and now he had to pour out every one of his secrets before it was too late.

A few weeks after his arrest, while trial preparation was still underway, the remains of little David Ferriera were found in an abandoned lot between a church and a supermarket. Dumped like so much garbage in a stained cardboard box. The head was missing, along with the majority of the internal organs, but there was enough intact for his mother to positively identify the body. Richard was confronted with the photographic evidence and casually confirmed that it was David, also. He had known exactly where the dead baby's body had been left, but instead of giving the family peace or ending the desperate hunt for it, he had chosen to keep that information to himself as it did not benefit him to share it.

The medication that had brought Richard's mania under control before his mother cut off the supply was administered to him daily in jail, yet as his sanity returned day by day, remorse never seemed to join it. He accepted that he had committed all the crimes that he was accused of, but he had no feelings about it. He was devoid of any feelings beyond the immediate. Pain, pleasure, and fear were all that he understood. The only stars to serve as his guide. Without his schizophrenia and paranoia to mask it, his lack of any internal world became ever more apparent.

Regardless of whether he would admit to being culpable for his crimes, there was no question that Rick had committed them, and there was ample evidence to place each murder firmly beyond any reasonable doubt. The legal system ambled forward into a trial.

The trial began on January 2, 1979, and lasted for four months as all of the evidence was brought out in a cavalcade of horrors. From the very beginning, Richard's plea was entered as 'not guilty by reason of insanity', but his defence could not provide a single psychiatric report that he had not been sane at the time of his crimes. Four separate analyses were performed, all with the same result. The subject's manipulation of the analyst indicated someone who was rational. With no hope of support from the medical community that he had spent so many decades plaguing, Richard's lawyer fell back on the history of mental illness, and Richard's time in mental hospitals, to support their claim that he was not competent at the time of the murders. Instead, Richard's history became another nail in his coffin as experts came forward to recount his obsession with killing, the dead birds found outside of his room, and the distinction between hallucinations, fixations, and actions, citing the fact that the overwhelming majority of schizophrenics never pose any danger to others.

Everywhere that Richard turned, he met another dead end. He reached out to Agent Robert Ressler, the man whose profile had helped to capture him, in the hope that the same keen psychological insight might spare him from facing the consequences of his actions, but Ressler was unsurprisingly reticent about chasing after Nazi conspiracies or UFOs that might prove Richard's innocence. He agreed readily to an extensive interview with Richard that might, hypothetically, aid in his appeal, but was unable to provide him with any viable excuses that might help him dodge sentencing.

Ressler's profile, indicating that Richard was a disorganised killer who likely did not plan his crimes in advance, was used to try and have the charges reduced to second-degree murder, but this, too, was discarded by the court. Richard's pattern of behaviour was consistent with someone planning to commit murders, even if the specific victims were not selected in advance.

After being bombarded constantly with the grotesquery of the evidence, the jury was more than ready to pronounce their verdict when the time came. On 8th May, they took only five hours to come to their conclusions and convict Richard of six counts of first-degree murder. The sentence for this crime was death.

Death of a Vampire

On death row in San Quentin, Richard found that his reputation preceded him. The inmates had heard all about the gruesome nature of his crimes, and they loathed him for them and feared him in equal measure. Everywhere that he went, he was bombarded with demands that he kill himself. None of the fearsome prisoners of San Quentin dared to approach him themselves, but they all wanted him dead nonetheless. It was here in prison that his nickname replaced his real name in reporting about his crimes, and he became widely known as The Vampire of Sacramento.

The program of medication meant to keep Richard's mental health on an even keel soon began to falter when he was expected to self-administer it, and with his hallucinations returning in full force, he was soon transferred out of the prison and into Vacaville State Hospital until his condition could be brought back under control. The state could not legally execute an insane man, so by taking the medication as directed and returning to reality, Richard was figuratively signing his own death sentence. It was unsurprising that he preferred to dwell in his fantasies rather than face the grim reality of the gas chamber.

The doctors in the hospital were horrified that Rick had been tried as competent at all, given the depth and breadth of his delusional state, but they were in no position to question the directives of the court. They did their job and got him back onto an even keel.

His stay in Vacaville was short-lived. Once he was placed on anti-depressants, his mental state soon evened out, leading the doctors to believe that it was simply the stress of imprisonment that was exacerbating his condition. He was returned to death row promptly after his 'sanity' returned.

While Rick's behaviour may have returned to something resembling normal, his internal world had opened out into a landscape of paranoia once more. He came to believe that he was being gassed and weakened every night while he slept. That his heart was shrinking once again. That the Nazi conspiracy that had been working against him his whole life had their hooks in the prison staff, and that his food was being poisoned.

Agent Ressler attended visits with Rick on a regular basis, working to compile information on his mental state to assist in the future pursuit and capture of similar criminals. In exchange for his compliance, Rick was afforded some small comforts that the other prisoners envied. Free cigarettes and extra furnishings in his cell marked him as one of San Quentin's resident celebrities, not to mention Ressler's constant campaigning to have him transferred out of the prison and into a dedicated mental healthcare facility. Yet still, Rick constantly pushed for more and more in return for his compliance in the interviews. At first, the demands were minor, but they soon escalated, in time with his return to his paranoid delusions. He wanted a radar gun. He believed that if he had a radar gun, he would be able to detect the UFOs that the Nazis were using to spy on him and prove that he was an innocent victim of their conspiracy. Ressler could not provide him with one, earning him Rick's ever-mounting suspicion that the lawman he was putting his trust into might be a counter-operative and that the FBI had been compromised by the conspiracy, too.

Each time that Ressler visited, he could see Rick becoming more desperate and frantic. He was absolutely convinced that he was being poisoned by the prison staff, and he needed Ressler to help him prove it. They were tampering with his meals, and they wouldn't let him visit the kitchens to see how the food was being prepared, or who was preparing it. Reaching into his pockets, Rick withdrew handfuls of macaroni and cheese that he had managed to smuggle out of the lunch hall. Pasta that he now tried to pass off to Ressler, demanding that the man test it for poisons and contaminants to prove his theories. Needless to say, Ressler was disgusted and horrified at the glutinous mass being thrust at him. He refused to take what the deranged inmate was offering him and terminated the interview when Rick persisted.

Richard would not consent to any further visits from Ressler after that point. He was no longer convinced that the FBI had his best interests at heart, or that the agent had any real interest in unravelling the conspiracy against him. With that last hope extinguished, Rick sank into an ever-deeper depression. Without a fresh infusion of blood, his heart was going to disappear soon. His glorious crusade and ascension to the realm of the living had been stopped almost as soon as it could begin. The system that was in place to grind all of humanity into compliance would not tolerate rebellion like his, but that did not mean that the fight for freedom was over. He may no longer serve the cause as a soldier pressing back against the Nazi UFO Conspiracy, but he could still be a martyr. Over the course of three weeks, he hid his three daily doses of Sinequan in his slip-on shoes, accumulating enough pills to constitute a lethal dose for a far larger man.

On the morning of the 26th of December, 1980, a correctional officer doing his rounds greeted Rick where he was lying normally in his bed in cell 5800. Rick was taciturn as he always was when he could see no advantage in speaking, but he gave a little wave of acknowledgement. An hour later, the same officer came back around and found Richard face down on the bed, his arms outstretched above his head. He was not responsive. Entering the cell carefully, the guard attempted to rouse Richard, only to discover that he was stiff and cold.

Medical staff were not summoned – there was no way to resuscitate the serial killer. Richard Chase was dead. Instead, the coroner, K. P. Holmes, was brought in to examine the scene of the death and certify it as self-inflicted.

The packets of Rick's pills were found stuffed under the mattress, and beside his bed were four sheets of paper, filled from margin to margin with his scribbled handwriting. Two of the pages were a rather conventional suicide note, detailing his plan to kill himself with hoarded pills. The other two were rather more in keeping with the man's nature. A square was drawn on each of the sheets, filled with symbols unknown to any earthly language. They formed a cryptographic puzzle, but one that was missing the one vital component required to solve it. The only key to the alien language written in the squares was in the poisoned brain of Richard Chase.

In the aftermath of his suicide, it was simply a procedure that Richard should receive a full autopsy, but there was a certain prurient interest in his remains among armchair criminologists who had heard stories about his delusions of sickness.

As it turned out, just as his many medical examinations through the years had proven, Richard had no abnormalities in his anatomy. There was no brain damage to explain his madness, no shrunken heart, no missing organs. The cause of death was toxic ingestion of the medication that he had hoarded, with a note linking that suicide to his long history of mental illness.

To this day, Richard Chase is the archetypal model that the FBI use when describing a disorganised killer. His one lasting legacy after thirty years of desperately fighting to survive all of his imaginary enemies was the lethal damage that his delusions had caused.

Want More?

Did you enjoy *Vampire Killer* and want some more True Crime?

YOUR FREE BOOK IS WAITING

From bestselling author Ryan Green

There is a man who is officially classed as **"Britain's most dangerous prisoner"**

The man's name is Robert Maudsley, and his crimes earned him the nickname **"Hannibal the Cannibal"**

This free book is an exploration of his story...

★ ★ ★ ★ ★ *"Ryan brings the horrifying details to life. I can't wait to read more by this author!"*

Get a free copy of **Robert Maudsley: Hannibal the Cannibal** when you sign up to join my Reader's Group.

www.ryangreenbooks.com/free-book

Every Review Helps

If you enjoyed the book and have a moment to spare, I would really appreciate a short review on Amazon. Your help in spreading the word is gratefully received and reviews make a huge difference to helping new readers find me. Without reviewers, us self-published authors would have a hard time!

Type in your link below to be taken straight to my book review page.

US	geni.us/vkUS
UK	geni.us/vkUK
Australia	geni.us/vkAUS
Canada	geni.us/vkCA

Thank you! I can't wait to read your thoughts.

About Ryan Green

Ryan Green is a true crime author who lives in Herefordshire, England with his wife, three children, and two dogs. Outside of writing and spending time with his family, Ryan enjoys walking, reading and windsurfing.

Ryan is fascinated with History, Psychology and True Crime. In 2015, he finally started researching and writing his own work and at the end of the year, he released his first book on Britain's most notorious serial killer, Harold Shipman.

He has since written several books on lesser-known subjects, and taken the unique approach of writing from the killer's perspective. He narrates some of the most chilling scenes you'll encounter in the True Crime genre.

You can sign up to Ryan's newsletter to receive a free book, updates, and the latest releases at:

WWW.RYANGREENBOOKS.COM

More Books by Ryan Green

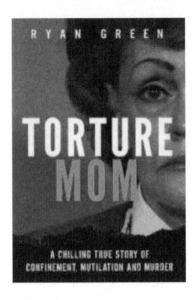

In July 1965, teenagers Sylvia and Jenny Likens were left in the temporary care of Gertrude Baniszewski, a middle-aged single mother and her seven children.

The Baniszewski household was overrun with children. There were few rules and ample freedom. Sadly, the environment created a dangerous hierarchy of social Darwinism where the strong preyed on the weak.
What transpired in the following three months was both riveting and chilling. The case shocked the entire nation and would later be described as "The single worst crime perpetuated against an individual in Indiana's history".

More Books by Ryan Green

On 29th February 2000, John Price took out a restraining order against his girlfriend, Katherine Knight. Later that day, he told his co-workers that she had stabbed him and if he were ever to go missing, it was because Knight had killed him.

The next day, Price didn't show up for work.

A co-worker was sent to check on him. They found a bloody handprint by the front door and they immediately contacted the police. The local police force was not prepared for the chilling scene they were about to encounter. Price's body was found in a chair, legs crossed, with a bottle of lemonade under his arm. He'd been decapitated and skinned. The "skin-suit" was hanging from a meat hook in the living room and his head was found in the kitchen, in a pot of vegetables that was still warm. There were two plates on the dining table, each had the name of one of Price's children on it.

She was attempting to serve his body parts to his children.

More Books by Ryan Green

In 1902, at the age of 11, Carl Panzram broke into a neighbour's home and stole some apples, a pie, and a revolver. As a frequent troublemaker, the court decided to make an example of him and placed him into the care of the Minnesota State Reform School. During his two-year detention, Carl was repeatedly beaten, tortured, humiliated and raped by the school staff.

At 15-years old, Carl enlisted in the army by lying about his age but his career was short-lived. He was dishonourably discharged for stealing army supplies and was sent to military prison. The brutal prison system sculpted Carl into the man that he would remain for the rest of his life. He hated the whole of mankind and wanted revenge.

When Carl left prison in 1910, he set out to rob, burn, rape and kill as many people as he could, for as long as he could. His campaign of terror could finally begin and nothing could stand in his way.

More Books by Ryan Green

In 1861, the police of a rural French village tore their way into the woodside home of Martin Dumollard. Inside, they found chaos. Paths had been carved through mounds of bloodstained clothing, reaching as high as the ceiling in some places.

The officers assumed that the mysterious maid-robber had killed one woman but failed in his other attempts. Yet, it was becoming sickeningly clear that there was a vast gulf between the crimes they were aware of and the ones that had truly been committed.

Would Dumollard's wife expose his dark secret or was she inextricably linked to the atrocities? Whatever the circumstances, everyone was desperate to discover whether the bloody garments belonged to some of the 648 missing women.

Free True Crime Audiobook

Listen to four chilling True Crime stories in one collection. Follow the link below to download a FREE copy of *The Ryan Green True Crime Collection: Vol. 3.*

WWW.RYANGREENBOOKS.COM/FREE-AUDIOBOOK

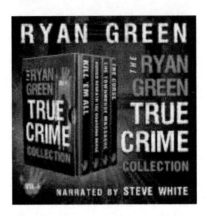

"Ryan Green has produced another excellent book and belongs at the top with true crime writers such as M. William Phelps, Gregg Olsen and Ann Rule" –**B.S. Reid**

"Wow! Chilling, shocking and totally riveting! I'm not going to sleep well after listening to this but the narration was fantastic. Crazy story but highly recommend for any true crime lover!" –**Mandy**

"Torture Mom by Ryan Green left me pretty speechless. The fact that it's a true story is just...wow" –**JStep**

"Graphic, upsetting, but superbly read and written" –**Ray C**

WWW.RYANGREENBOOKS.COM/FREE-AUDIOBOOK